Is God the Only Reality?

BY JOHN MARKS TEMPLETON

Discovering the Laws of Life

Evidence of Purpose (editor)

Looking Forward (editor)

Riches for the Mind and Spirit (editor)

The Templeton Plan (with James Ellison)

Global Investing the Templeton Way
(with Norman Berryessa and Eric Kirzner)

The God Who Would Be Known
(with Robert L. Herrmann)

The Humble Approach

Is God the Only Reality?

*Science Points to
a Deeper Meaning of the Universe*

John Marks Templeton
and
Robert L. Herrmann

Continuum • New York

1994
The Continuum Publishing Company
370 Lexington Avenue, New York, NY 10017

Printed in the United States of America

Library of Congress Cataloging-in-Publication Data

Templeton, John, 1912-
    Is God the only reality: science points to a deeper meaning of the universe / John Marks Templeton and Robert Herrmann.
        p.   cm.
        Includes bibliographic references and index.
        ISBN 0-8264-0650-5
        1. Religion and science. 2. God. I. Herrmann, Robert L., 1928- II. Title.
BL240.2.T434 1994
215—dc20   94-881
                                                                                CIP

Contents

Introduction

Is God the Only Reality?

The search for reality has reached a fever pitch in our Western society, with all sorts of conflicting voices shouting for their exclusive right to define "what's for real." But within this cacophony, two voices continue to dominate, to gain a major share of the audience. One is the time-honored voice of religion, the other the newer, younger voice of science.

Religion has been a part of the human experience from the very beginning, and it remains the most general characteristic of *Homo sapiens* in every culture—whether highly developed or relatively primitive. England's Arthur Peacocke says of mankind's religious experience:

> Ever since the emerging species of *Homo sapiens* started burying its dead with ritual, mankind has displayed an awareness of the tragedy of the ephemeral, the Reality and yet the inner unacceptability of the cycle of life and death, and has sought a transcendent meaning in another reality for that brief flickering into self-consciousness which all its members experience. Thus the religious quest, the long search for meaning and significance, is one of the most characteristic features of all societies—and I do not exclude our own, for there are rooms waiting to be filled by God in the interior castle of every Western soul.[1]

When we turn to examine the impact of science upon our culture, the overwhelming conclusion must be that we are heavily indebted to a scientific way of thinking and reliant upon the technology that science has so richly provided. Indeed, from its very beginnings, science has brought wonderful things to our eyes. For Galileo it was sunspots and Jupiter's moons. For Isaac Newton it was the force of gravity and the dance of heavenly bodies. For James Maxwell it was electromagnetism, a mysterious attraction acting without benefit of springs or pulleys. For Albert Einstein, it was light with immutable speed, which placed time and space at risk, no longer absolute and now inseparable. For James Watson and Francis Crick it was DNA, the genetic stuff, life's information stored in giant paired helices. For Stephen Hawking and Robert Penrose it was the Big Bang, the beginning of our universe, and of our own cosmic evolution.

With these and innumerable other discoveries has come the temptation to beleive that we are that Prometheus who stole fire from the Gods, whom Leonardo da Vinci portrayed with the many arms of the technological wizard. It is a grand time for the toolmaker—gene splicing, space exploration, artificial intelligence.

In some sense the technological advances have given meaning to our scientific culture, but there still remains that deep desire for meaning, for a cosmic explanation of ourselves. For in all our scientific understanding of our world, what we are and how we have come to be yet eludes us. And the most astounding thing is that this ignorance is characteristic of all our exploration. It seems that the deeper we probe into the nature of things, the more complex and mysterious they become. It could be that this is a transient experience, and that the future will bring everything into focus. It may be that, as George Field and Eric Chaisson have it in their preface to *The Invisible Universe*: "We are in a period of grand technological progress, a time of learning, of groping in the darkness—more a time of exploration than of mature science."[2]

It may be that this is only a stage we are passing through, with full understanding awaiting us down the line. But we think not. We have written this book to tell why, to describe the current state of some of the frontiers of physical and biological science, and to show how the exploration leads in each case to a greater mystery with ever deeper and more profound implications about what is real. What we see gradually coming into focus will be a surprise for many. We conclude that the only coherent explanation, the grand organizing paradigm, to which both science and religion point but which neither begins to exhaust, is the God of the universe— what Loren Eiseley called "the Great Face Behind."[3]

Since this is a book about science and religion, the reader will encounter technical sections that we deem important for the scientifically and theologically sophisticated. For other readers, we believe most of the technical sections can be skimmed quickly without losing the thread of the argument. For example, in the chapter on particle physics, the details of quarks and leptons and bosons is provided to illustrate the extreme difficulty of obtaining a full description of physical reality, but comprehension of the complexity is not essential.

Overall, we hope this book will astound you with the way in which reality has eluded both scientists and theologians and we hope some of you will be moved to begin the exploration into a deeper understanding of the ways of God with all of his creatures in the long history of this cosmos. The manifold scientific discoveries of the late twentieth century cause the visible and tangible to appear less and less real and point to a greater reality in the ongoing and accelerating creative process within the enormity of the vast unseen.

1

The Changing Faces of Reality

I. The Changing Character of Physical Reality

We live in a world of change, and nowhere is that more pronounced than in the sciences. Indeed, a textbook unrevised for two or three years is practically useless in most fields, and a laboratory with ten-year-old equipment is a museum. But most scientists are quick to point out that some things in science are far more secure—the periodic table, the laws of thermodynamics, relativity, the genetic code, biological evolution—and that we are steadily building a foundation of unchanging fact from which a clear picture of physical reality is emerging.

Not everyone agrees with this expectation, however, even within the scientific community. In fact, among the growing group of scientists interested in the philosophical implications of science, it has become apparent that we can no longer talk about scientific concepts and even mechanisms as though they were literal descriptions of objective reality.

A. NAIVE TO CRITICAL REALISM

In his book *Intimations of Reality*, Arthur Peacocke tells us that from about 1920 until 1970 science was viewed as an "essentially logical enterprise" through which the external world could be exhaustively described.[1] Peacocke quotes Mary Hesse's version of the earlier view in *Revolutions and Reconstructions in the Philosophy of Science*:

> Science is ideally a linguistic system in which true propositions are in one-to-one relation to facts, including facts that are not directly observed be-

cause they involve hidden entities or properties, or past events or far distant events. These hidden events are described in theories, and theories can be inferred from observation, that is, the hidden explanatory mechanism of the world can be discovered from what is open to observations. Man as scientist is regarded as standing apart from the world and able to experiment and theorize about it objectively and dispassionately.[2]

Mary Hesse goes on to explain that the developments of the past two decades have made this description appear exceedingly naive. Indeed, every part of this account has been brought into question. A forerunner in this critique of science is Thomas Kuhn, whose *Structure of Scientific Revolutions*, published in 1970, proposed a new interpretation of the history of science.[3] Kuhn argues that science goes through periods of normality during which accepted paradigms—broad conceptual frameworks—are employed and applied, and periods of revolution in which these paradigms are shattered, and replaced by new ones. The implications of this picture for our understanding of physical reality are far-reaching. If this be true of science, there seems little hope that the "hidden explanatory mechanisms of the world" can be discovered. A simple convergence to a unique scientific truth seems highly unlikely.

Following Kuhn, a new emphasis was placed on the sociological factors influencing the development of science, an analysis of which turned out to be as complicated as the scientists themselves. As Arthur Peacocke describes it:

> Science came to be seen as a continuous social enterprise, and the rise and fall of theories and the use and replacement of concepts as involving a complex of personal, social, intellectual, and cultural interactions that often determined whether a theory was accepted or rejected. Theories are constructed, it was argued, in terms of the prevailing "world view" of the scientists involved: so to understand them one must understand the relevant world view. A new emphasis was therefore placed on the history of science, especially the sociological factors influencing its development. Thus a new area was opened up for the application of the expanding enterprise of the sociology of knowledge in general and of scientific knowledge in particular. However, it turns out that the "world view" of the scientist is an exceedingly complex and elusive entity—even more so when a *community* of scientists is involved.[4]

Some sociologists of science concluded that the physical world has little to do with the conclusions arrived at by the scientific community. In essence, the products of science are social constructions like any other products of culture.

This extreme view finds many critics in and out of the scientific community. One of the most effective spokesmen for scientific reality is philosopher Ernan McMullin, who has argued for uniqueness in scientific truth gathering. He points out that even though science is a social product, the social factors are limited by the unique corrective character of scientific activity. The continuous filtering and sifting that go on in the course of experimental collaboration and scientific interaction and publication lead to a progressive elimination of distortion.[5] McMullin has also commented on the "fertility" of scientific theories in further support of their realistic status. A good scientific theory in his view is able to predict novel phenomena and new directions. It has what he calls "logical resources." It also has another resource, a subtle capacity to suggest modifications when predictions fail, thereby providing a creative move for the scientist. In this respect McMullin compares the scientific theory or model with the poet's metaphor, which he describes as follows:

> The poet uses a metaphor not just as decoration but as a means of expressing a complex thought. A good metaphor has its own sort of precision, as any poet will tell you. It can lead the mind in ways that literal language cannot. The poet who is developing a metaphor is led by suggestion, not by implication; the reader of the poem queries the metaphor and searches among its many resonances for the ones that seem best to bear insight. The simplistic "man is a wolf" examples of metaphor have misled philosophers into supposing that what is going on in metaphor is a comparison between two already partly understood things. The only challenge then would be to decide in what respect the analogy holds. In the more complex metaphors of modern poetry, something much more interesting is happening. The metaphor is helping to illuminate something that is not well understood in advance, perhaps, some aspect of human life that we find genuinely puzzling or frightening or mysterious. The manner in which such metaphors work is by tentative suggestion. The minds of poet and reader alike are actively engaged in creating.[6]

The comparison of the creativity of scientific theory and poetic metaphor brings to mind the special contribution that scientist-philosopher Michael Polanyi has made to our appreciation of the belief system of the scientist.[7] To raise the question of belief might seem to provide one more salient argument for the social scientists, but Polanyi's analysis arrives at the astounding conclusion that the scientist's commitment to the essential truth he is seeking actually serves as a valid and even essential component in approaching reality. The social context, at least at the personal level, actually ensures that the scientist is moving toward reality. Further discussion of this aspect can also be found in our book, *The God Who Would Be Known*.[8]

The debates between extremists arguing for scientific reality as purely social construction and those arguing for science as final truth has led to a good compromise referred to as the critical realist position, which McMullin describes as follows:

> The basic claim made by scientific realism. . . is that the long-term success of a scientific theory gives reason to believe that something like the entities and structure postulated in the theory actually exist. There are four important qualifications built into this: (1) the theory must be a successful one over a significant period; (2) the explanatory success of the theory gives some reason, though not a conclusive warrant, to believe [it]; (3) what is believed is that the theoretical structures are *something like* the structures of the real; (4) no claim is made for a special, more basic, privileged, form of existence for the postulated entities.[9]

According to Peacocke, the qualifications ("significant period," "some kind," "something like") built into this description are essential to a defense of scientific realism. Working scientists understand the extent and nature of provisionality that is assigned to theories in their field.

Their proposed theories and models are understood as no more than approximations of the structures of reality. Nevertheless, there is often an increasing sense of confidence that reality is being more and more accurately described, especially as that knowledge is successfully applied in prediction and control and in the design of new experiments. This description Peacocke refers to as "a skeptical and qualified realism." [10]

To illustrate this approach to scientific realism, Peacocke takes the example of the electron. Scientists are committed to "believing in" the electron on the basis of much experimental data. However, "what they believe" about electrons has undergone many changes, but they still refer by way of long social links to the entity described in that historical event when the electron was first discovered. Physicists believe in the existence of electrons but are reluctant to say what they are. But "they are always open to new ways of thinking about them that will enhance the reliability of future predictions and render their understanding more comprehensive." [11]

But what makes the electron most believable by the physicist is that it functions as a tool. Despite the fact that the electron cannot be observed, it can regularly be manipulated to investigate other aspects of nature. Peacocke calls this "the experimental argument for realism," pointing out that it deals with entities rather than theories.[12] To illustrate the experimental argument, Peacocke quotes Ian Hacking in *Representing and Intervening* as follows:

> There are surely innumerable entities and processes that humans will never know about. Perhaps there are many that in principle we can never know about. Reality is bigger than us. The best kinds of evidence for the reality of a postulated or inferred entity is that we can begin to measure it or otherwise understand its causal powers. The best evidence, in turn, that we have this kind of understanding is that we can set out, from scratch, to build machines that will work fairly reliably, taking advantage of this or that causal nexus. Hence, engineering, not theorizing, is the best proof of scientific realism about entities.[13]

It should be noted that this argument points up a significant weakness in recent speculations by theoretical physicists in connection with the grand unified theories. These theories, which seek to bring the forces of the universe into a single coherent structure, are highly speculative and for the most part unsubstantiated by empirical data. There is here what physicist Richard Morris calls a "widening gap between theory and experiment" and a consequent "risk of putting forth questions that are unverifiable, and therefore meaningless."[14]

B. SCIENTIFIC MODELS

Earlier we alluded to the way in which scientific theorizing and model building had its counterpart in the poet's metaphor. Arthur Peacocke tells us that, strictly speaking, the metaphor can only be a figure of speech, in which we speak of one thing in terms that suggest some other thing.[15] On the other hand, a model need not be linguistic, though the two may be closely linked, since metaphors arise when we speak about our models. For example, the use of the computer as a model for the brain elicits the metaphors of "programming," "input," "feedback," and "memory."

As we have seen, the poet's metaphor helps to illuminate that which is not well understood by tentative suggestion, leaving the reader to create ideas and images from what is given in another more familiar form. The scientific model performs a similar function in that it generates metaphorical theoretical terms that suggest a network of explanation. Scientific theories are built by construction of models, and good models are not only inseparable from their theories, but allow for theory development by suggesting new possibilities and accommodating new observations. "A model," Janet Soskice says in her book *Metaphor and Religious Language*, "is the living part of the theory, the cutting edge of its projective capacity and, hence,…indispensable for explanatory and predictive purposes."[16]

Arthur Peacocke points out that there is not total agreement on the essential role of the model in scientific theorizing. Some scientists and philosophers regard models as helpful but carrying no commitment concerning their relation to reality. But the majority take a critical realist approach and see models as essential and permanent features of science. However, he points out that the critical realist *sees* the model as only a partial and incomplete expression of reality, a construction that no one would view as final truth. The use of complementary models in science, such as the wave and particle models for light in physics, should serve to remind us that models can never be literal and always contain some inadequacy.[17]

In agreement with Peacocke, physicist Richard Morris, in his book *The Nature of Reality*, points out that by the end of the nineteenth century, physicists were viewing scientific theories as approximations that were only models of reality though sometimes very good ones. He comments: "Theories bore the same relation to the physical world that an architect's model did to a building, or that a detailed drawing did to a scene in nature. The correspondence between model and reality might be very close, but it could never be exact."[18] But the reasons for the present conservative point of view on the part of most physicists stems from the fact that the entities that are studied are rarely seen directly and only inferred from various kinds of observed phenomena. One cannot see gravitational fields or the curvature of space-time, and even an electron must be inferred from the spot of light it leaves on a fluorescent screen or the track of tiny bubbles of hydrogen gas that a beam of electrons leaves in a bubble chamber.

The theoretical physicist devises theories about the behavior of these particles, but if theoretical predictions are subsequently confirmed by experiment, one still has not demonstrated their real existence. All that can be said is that the model conforms reasonably well to reality. It does not exclude the possibility of other models or other refinements of the present one. In fact, Morris says, in every field of physics there are experimental results that do not agree with theoretical predictions at all. Often these anomalous results are ignored and sometimes they later prove to be the result of faulty experimentation. However, occasionally they prove to be fundamental, explainable only when whole new theories are developed.[19]

Despite this long history of revision and rebuilding of the models of physics, Morris tells us that some present-day scientists are suggesting that their models are approaching perfection, a point of view that was characteristic of the age of Isaac Newton, who thought it was possible to discover exact laws of nature.[20] The current proposal of a theory of quantum gravity by Stephen Hawking as described in his book *A Brief History of Time* seeks to join the four forces of nature into a single unified theory.[21] Hawking is so intrigued by the all-inclusiveness of the theory and its apparent capacity to explain the early stages of the origin of the universe that he equates quantum gravity with physical reality. This hope was expressed at the time of his inaugural lecture as Lucasian Professor of Mathematics at Cambridge in 1980; ironically, he was assuming the chair once occupied by Sir Isaac Newton.[22]

Not everyone in physics is happy with Hawking's idea that a complete theory will be found. Morris goes on to explain that Freeman Dyson of Princeton's Institute for Advanced Study is one such dissenter. Dyson has commented: "If it should turn out that the whole of physical reality can be described by a finite set of equations, I would be very disappointed. I would feel that the Creator had been uncharacteristically lacking in imagination."[23] Dyson goes on to say that it is more likely that the laws of physics are inexhaustible, basing his argument on the famous theorem of the Czech mathematician Kurt Gödel. Gödel's theorem, which was proved in 1931, states that it is not possible to demonstrate that any mathematical system is both consistent and complete. If the system is consistent, then it cannot be complete; there must exist true statements that cannot be proved within the system. Statements of this kind are referred to as *undecidable* and a number of them have been described. Most mathematicians agree that because of this limitation on mathematical systems—which could be viewed as mathematical *models*—Gödel proved that mathematics is inexhaustible. It might be said that its models will never be complete. Dyson concludes that because of Gödel's theorem, mathematics will always have "fresh questions to ask and fresh ideas to discover," and he hopes that physics will prove to be just as inexhaustible.[24]

American physicist John Wheeler is another critic of the idea that any mathematical formulation such as quantum gravity can be a full description of physical reality. He argues against the idea of "a magic equation," and goes on to make the very important point that much of the formulation of the unification of forces is theoretical and devoid of experimental support.

As he expresses it: "What we call 'reality' consists of an elaborate papier-mâché construction of imagination and theory filled in between a few iron posts of observation."[25]

C. SCIENCE AS A HIERARCHY OF SYSTEMS

Not only is the tendency ever present in science for theory to far exceed observation, but scientists are often guilty of reductionism. Arthur Peacocke tells us in his book *God and the New Biology* that scientific methodologies are powerful and effective because they involve the resolution of complex structure into simpler components. However, the success of this reductionism at the methodological level often carries over into a more general philosophical attitude. In the case of biology, for example, one finds biologists saying that living organisms are "nothing but" a physicochemical system, and some sociobiologists saying that all social behavior is explainable on a biological basis. Over against this attitude, Peacocke argues for an appreciation of the distinctiveness of the various scientific disciplines as an ascending arrangement or hierarchy of systems. For example, in the progression from physics to chemistry to biology to ecology each succeeding science becomes enriched in empirical content and new concepts emerge at each level that simply are not present in the preceding levels. Statements that are true of the lower levels are also true of the higher ones, though the lower-level statements are usually not the focus of interest for scientists working in the higher-level disciplines. However, concepts appear at the higher level that have no definition at the lower. For example, British biophysicist Donald MacKay points out, in his *Clockwork Image*, that a term from biology like *adaptation* has no definition in physics and chemistry.[27] Likewise, Peacocke takes the illustration of biological information. Our knowledge of the physicochemical nature of genetic material in the form of deoxyribonucleic acid is a salient contribution from chemistry, but the concept of information flow is a function and property of the whole organism and so is necessarily restricted to the level of biology or above. Reductionism thus is not appropriate at the level of theory. We can be reductionist in methodology but not in epistemology. Theories are autonomous.[28] The picture has been described well by French molecular biologist François Jacob, who refers to the integrated subunits at each level of the hierarchy as integrons. Integrons of each higher level are made up by the assembly of the various integrons of the preceding level:

> From particles to man there is a whole series of integration, of levels, of discontinuities. But there is no breach either in the composition of the objects or in the reactions that take place in them; no change in "essence." So much so, that investigation of molecules and cellular organelles has now become the concern of physicists....This does not at all mean that biology has become an annex of physics, that it represents as it were, a junior branch concerned with complex systems. At each level of organization, novelties appear in both properties and logic. To reproduce is not within the power of any single molecule by itself. This faculty appears only with the simplest integron deserving to be called a living organism, that is, the cell. But thereafter the rules of the game change. At the higher-level integron, the cell population, natural selection imposes new constraints and offers new possibilities. In this way, and without ceasing to obey the principles that govern inanimate systems, living systems become subject to phenomena that have no meaning at the lower level. *Biology can neither be reduced to physics, nor do without it.* Every object that biology studies is a system of systems. Being part of a higher-order system itself, it sometimes obeys rules that cannot be deduced simply by analyzing it. This means that each level of organization must be considered with reference to the adjacent levels.... At every level of integration, some new characteristics come to light....Very often, concepts and techniques that apply at one level do not function either above or below it. The various levels of biological organization are united by the logic proper to reproduction. They are distinguished by the means of communication, the regulatory circuits and the internal logic proper to each system.[29]

The consequences of the existence of the hierarchies of complexity are threefold, according to Peacocke. One interesting consequence is that we see the natural world as an evolved hierarchy in which new kinds of more complex organization have arisen from simpler systems over the vast periods of time and by distinct developmental steps in which each preceding system was precursor to that following.[30] The second consequence aims directly at the question of reality, since it has often been assumed by reductionists that explanations at the level of atoms and molecules are the only "real" or valued explanations. The realization that an enrichment of our understanding of reality follows with each succeeding order of complexity, which is not reducible to its predecessor, and which brings new concepts and methodologies to the descriptive process, greatly broadens our view of reality. As Peacocke says: "There is no sense in which subatomic particles are to be graded as 'more real' than, say, a bacterial cell or a human person or, even, social facts. Each level has to be regarded as a cut through the totality of reality, if you like, in the sense that we have to take account of its mode of operation at that level."[31]

A third consequence of the existence of hierarchies is that a structure is suggested for the interrelationship between scientific and theological views of reality.

II. Theology and Changing Reality

Just as the last few decades of the twentieth century have brought vast changes to our understanding of the physical reality we approach through science, so also a major upheaval has been experienced in our understanding of the reality of God that religion provides and theology interprets. Support for religious experience as a widely shared approach to reality has been provided by the studies of William James[32] and Alistair Hardy.[33] Hardy researched the religious experiences of a broad spectrum of British society and concluded that religion is deeply rooted in human nature and experienced at every level of economic status and educational background. Indeed, some outstanding scientists have expressed the importance of a religious experience as an essential part of their appreciation of science. Philosopher Michael Polanyi had noted that scientific truth seeking involved a commitment to truth not unlike religious belief.[34] Physicist Albert Einstein displayed an especially sensitive attitude toward the religious experience, as recorded by Lincoln Barnet in his *The Universe and Dr. Einstein*. Einstein says:

> The most beautiful and most profound emotion we can experience is the sensation of the mystical. It is the sower of all true science. He to whom this emotion is a stranger, who can no longer wonder and stand rapt in awe, is as good as dead. To know that what is impenetrable to us really exists, manifesting itself as the highest wisdom and the most radiant beauty which our dull faculties can comprehend only in their most primitive forms—this knowledge, this feeling is at the center of true religiousness.[35]

German physicist Werner Heisenberg, in his book *Physics and Beyond*, speaks of "the central order," the "one" with which we communicate in the language of religion. For Heisenberg, the very idea of truth is bound up in the reality of religious experience.[36] Anthropologist Loren Eiseley, in his *The Firmament of Time*, looks sensitively at our Neanderthal ancestors, especially at their burial practices, and concludes that even 300,000 years ago men like ourselves gently laid their dead in sepulchers with the expectation that "the grave is not the end." [37]

Indeed, it is our conviction that the religious quest for meaning and purpose in another, transcendent Reality is the common experience in every culture and every age since the emergence of humankind.[38]

But Peacocke reminds us that, in the current climate of rapid change, theological interpretation has to take into account a strong move in every culture toward material necessity, toward fulfillment in this present world as human beings who are linked closely to the natural world and to each other.[39] Stewardship of the environment and ethical concerns about technological innovation have become major issues for the religious community. Then, too, there have come changes in our attitude toward the authority of Scripture and of the various religious traditions. Indeed, the social critiques that have been directed at science have their counterpart in the religious communities. How much of the truth of Scripture and tradition is culturally conditioned and how much is absolutely authoritative? Much of the ferment has led to a renewed interest in the nature of theological reality, and to an awareness that science and theology have a number of interesting similarities.

A. THEOLOGICAL MODELS AND REALITY

Peacocke points out that just as scientific realism has gone through a transition from the naive realism of the positivist to the critical realist position of the socially sensitive scientific skeptic, so also theology has experienced a healthy reassessment of the nature of theological doctrine and acquired a valuable perspective on the use of theological language as model and metaphor. The naive realism of the scientist has its counterpart in the fundamentalist literalism of the theologian, and the critical realist position in science would be comparable to a theological viewpoint that regarded the doctrines and symbols of theology as partial and limited but nevertheless essential ways of expressing the reality that is God and God's relation to human beings.[40]

The recognition that religious and theological language is a form of expression that depends upon models was first emphasized by Ian Ramsey in his book *Models and Mystery, Models for Divine Activity, and Religious Language.*[41] What has been appreciated is that the Scriptures make extensive use of models. God is described as Father, Creator, King, Shepherd, Judge. Jesus is described as the Christ, the Second Adam, the Great Physician, the Son, the Lamb. The third person of the Trinity is figured as Holy Spirit, Holy Ghost, Comforter. And the Trinity itself is a quite metaphorical construction—God as Creator, Incarnate as the Son, and Immanent as the Holy Spirit. God's relationship to the world is often depicted by monarchical models (God as King, Sovereign, Maker) or by organic models (the created order as a garment worn by God, or as the work of a potter, or as the emanation of life-giving energy, or as the spoken word). The atonement through Christ's death is described in terms of models such as sacrifice, redemption, ransom, and substitution.

Just as in the case of scientific models, theological models are analogical and metaphorical, rather than attempting to be explicitly descriptive or literal. Here again the idea of discovery and increasing intelligibility is involved, but the subject is the relationship nature-man-God. The context for discovery for both scientific and theological models is a community with what Peacocke calls "a living tradition of reference back to originating experiments and experiences, and one that has developed and is still developing language to maintain this continuity of intelligibility."[42]

In science, the continuous linguistic community provides the essential social structure through which discovery of entities and establishment of terminology occurs. By comparison, in the Christian community, for example, key terms and concepts relate back to statements in the biblical sources or statements by church councils convened to formulate—often after heated debate—the valid interpretation and language (the appropriate models) of theology. Furthermore, these experiences of God continue to occur and to be the subject of interpretation as new findings of a historical or scientific type impact on theological models.

Finally, there are areas in which theology, as an expression of the nature-man-God relationship, goes beyond the models and metaphors of science. For example, if we examine theology's place in the kind of hierarchy of systems we discussed for the categories of science, we discover that theology stands apart, or above, the various sciences because of its highly integrative approach.

In Arthur Peacocke's words:

> In human religious activities, whole persons interact with each other, with the natural world, and with the transcendent, yet immanent, Creator as the source of all that is—the One who, for the theist, gives them and the

world meaning and ultimate significance. No higher level of integrated relationships in the hierarchy of natural systems can be envisaged, and theology is about the conceptual schemes (theories) and models and associated metaphors that articulate the content of this activity of the individual and of a historical community. So it should not be surprising if its theories, models, and metaphors turn out to be uniquely specific to, and characteristic of, this emergent level.

Thus we can have a legitimate placement for the activity and language of the theological enterprise as it reflects on this specifically and uniquely human activity that, involving nature, man, and God in its total integrating purview, stands at the summit of conceivable complexity and wholeness. Perhaps theology, if no longer the medieval "queen of the sciences," may at least be accorded the honors of a constitutional monarch?" [43]

B. Affective and Cognitive Factors in Approaching Reality

Whether or not the relationship between scientific and theological reality is any longer a royal one, it seems evident to us that science and theology have much to offer each other as complementary avenues to truth. However, Peacocke points out that some philosophers have distinguished religious models from scientific ones by the strong affective character of the former. It is noted that writers like Thomas Faucett in *The Symbolic Language of Religion* have suggested that theological models have more of a "participator" character since they evoke personal feelings—moral and spiritual response—whereas scientific models are of an "observer" type because they function in a more cognitive role to explain, represent, and predict. [44] Some authors have carried this distinction to the extreme by implying that the reality depicted by theological models is simply an awareness of the human condition and the need for faith and trust. But, as Janet Soskice suggests, faith requires an object, and theological models stir the will and emotions because of their cognitive content with respect to a transcendent Reality. Without the cognitive content they would not respond as they do. As she says:

> Typically Christians respond to the models of their religious tradition not because they take them to be elegant and compelling means of describing the human condition but because they believe them in some way to depict states and relations of a transcendent kind.... In practice, Christians tend to regard their models as both explanatory and reality depicting; and, although the basis from which a model may claim to depict reality differs between religious models and scientific ones, their application as explanatory is not as different as has been suggested. [45]

Arthur Peacocke goes on to compare the way in which models in science and theology are arrived at, and concludes that as with science, theological models depend for their development upon a social chain of reference and a body of repeatable experience. The chain of reference is founded in a body of "initiating experiences" at the time of "introducing events," and is then communicated through a continuous chain of repeated and new experiences that enable us to refer now to that to which the initiators referred. In this process, our models may have been revised through continuous reinterpretation, in the "development of doctrine," and some interpreters and communities may have acquired more authority than others, but the congruences of current experiences with earlier ones provide "guides to bring harmony to the cacophony of voices that claim to speak of that reality which is God." [46] The thrust of this view of theological development is that both science and theology have a heavy contribution from the cognitive side, in which reference back to formative historical events and continuous experimental application and testing are major model-building factors in the approach to reality.

Thus it might be concluded that there is more of a balance of affective and cognitive components in both scientific and theological models of reality, with perhaps the affective favored in theology and the cognitive in science. But what must be reemphasized is that the scientific models are surely not devoid of the affective, more personal components, for it is people who do science, and scientists who are now probing the deepest philosophical-theological questions about the nature of the universe and the nature of human beings. As we will discuss in the next chapter, there is much talk about God in cosmologist Stephen Hawking's *A Brief History of Time* in which he proposes a theory of quantum gravity to unite the forces of the universe. The traditional separation between the how of science and the why of theology is becoming more and more blurred as we probe the very foundations of nature. But it is not just in our day that scientists have sought for "bigger game." Throughout his career, Albert Einstein retained a passion to know the mind of God, to know nature as to intent and purpose. The search for a unified field theory occupied much of his later intellectual life. Edinburgh theologian Thomas Torrance tells us that Einstein had a deep sense of the harmony between the human mind, with all its limitations, and the rationality embedded in the universe, and he felt that the unification of the forces of the universe would explain "why it is what it is and not something else." [47]

Science is not only invading the provinces of the "why" and thereby demonstrating its affective character, but it is also entering the realm of the "ought," the domain of ethics, another very personal concern. The American biologist Edward Wilson has become the leading theoretician of the new science of sociobiology, which he defines as the "systematic study of the biological basis of all social behavior." In his book *Sociobiology, the New Synthesis*, Wilson proposes that human behavior is strongly determined by genetic elements, and that the particular activity of ethical reflection is a part of that genetic conditioning.[48] From an evolutionary perspective, those ethical patterns have been selected that were most adaptive to the survival and reproductive success of the species. As Philip Hefner discusses in his article "Is/Ought: A Risky Relationship between Theology and Science,"[49] sociobiologists propose that the human evolutionary record contains not only the description of the structural transition of the various human subspecies, but also records their "oughts," their ethical propensities, which have been chosen in the past and handed down to us. The proposal that our moral choices are built into our genes seems profoundly challenging to the theological model of a human moral structure made in some sense in God's image. Perhaps sociobiologists will become the high priests of a new religion of the future. Perhaps it will turn out that moral values have arisen in an "emergent" way in the course of evolution, still leaving us with a less than ultimate explanation.

But there may also be another reason for scientists to be concerned about ethics. Torrance reminds us of Einstein's demand that science be concerned with the "inner justification of natural law." Just as commitment to the reality of truth compels us to bring truth to light, that commitment also compels us to seek to enhance the order of a universe whose ultimate ground is order. This, Torrance says, is "a moral imperative latent in reality itself," and compels us to interact with nature not just in accordance with what things *actually are* but in accordance with what they *ought to be.*"[50]

Summary

We have sought to focus in this chapter on the complexity and limited precision of both scientific and theological expressions of reality. Both disciplines use models and metaphors to deal with this complexity, and there is both affective and cognitive content in both scientific and theological models. It is especially interesting that recent developments in cosmology and sociobiology have led science into a more general openness to discuss possible theological and ethical correlates to scientific models.

We are tempted to see this movement in more positive terms than do many in science and theology, because the interpenetration of the categories of "how" and "why" and of "is" and "ought" may well bring science and theology together again as joint participants in understanding what Einstein called the "inner justification of natural law" and Heisenberg called "the central order." Perhaps, in the end, Reality will appear far deeper and more profound than our limited human abilities can ever hope to comprehend.

2

Particles, Fields, and Reality

I f physical models or theories are only approximations or reflections of reality, and if their validity is heavily dependent upon experimental or observational verification, then it would seem appropriate to look in more detail at the way the experimental component is arrived at. In this chapter we have chosen to focus on the experimental approach to matter in the form in which the physicist encounters it, as particles and fields, to see what has been found out about its nature.

I. A Brief History of Subatomic Physics

Physicists are inclined to say that the universe is constructed of quantum fields, and that subatomic particles are only manifestations of fields. The reason given for this is that it is mathematically easier to describe the stuff of the universe in terms of electromagnetic and gravitational fields than to deal with each of the many different kinds of particles. Yet, for the most part it is particles that are studied in the laboratory. These are the "iron posts of observation" of reality.[1] The history of experimental physics is the history of the discovery of electrons, protons, neutrons, and some two hundred other subatomic particles. It began with the discovery of the electron by J. J. Thomson is 1897. This was followed by the English physicist Ernest Rutherford's discovery of the atomic nucleus in 1911 and the revelation that if nuclei were bombarded with alpha particles, they broke up to yield, among other things, the nuclei of hydrogen atoms. These "protons," as they were later called, were therefore assumed to be the fundamental constituents of the nucleus. Richard Morris tells us that these two particles, together with photons, were thought to provide an explanation for all the phenomena of physics. Following this, the picture was developed that all of the elements were built by successive additions of protons to the nucleus and a corresponding number of electrons, half of them in the nucleus and half revolving in orbits outside the nucleus.

Later, in the mid-1920s, quantum mechanics was developed, and with it came a sudden convulsion within the physics community. According to the formulations of quantum mechanics, electrons could not be confined to the nucleus. By this time, a number of other peculiar characteristics of the electron had been described. In 1905 the German physicist Max Planck had discovered that radiation from a heated object was emitted only in discrete packets, or quanta. An object could not emit any less than one quanta of energy in a given period of time. A threshold existed that seemed to specify that energy could not be divided below a certain amount. This observation was baffling to Planck, because of the already-established picture of light as a wave phenomenon. By analogy, it was as though an ocean wave could contain only certain numbers of cubic feet of water that were multiples of some discrete unit of water. But German physicist Albert Einstein published a paper in agreement with Planck's formulation in 1905, the same year Einstein published his paper on special relativity. He had been studying the photoelectric effect, the phenomenon in which electrons were ejected from certain metals by an incident beam of light. He discovered that the production of electrons was dependent upon the frequency of the light, and that below a critical value no electrons were produced. The light bombarding the metal surface appeared to be behaving like discrete packets—waves of particles. It seemed that light was made up of particles.

Planck's quantum theory of radiation formed a significant foundation for Danish physicist Niels Bohr's quantum theory of the atom, published in 1913. Bohr proposed that only certain specific orbits were possible for electrons in the atom, and that atoms could absorb energy only in amounts (quanta) that corresponded to jumps between orbits.

These ideas seemed to suggest that electrons might also have the wave-like character of light, but it was not until 1924 that French physicist Louis de Broglie presented in his doctoral dissertation a theory of electron waves. Two years later the Austrian physicist Erwin Schrödinger elaborated on de Broglie's hypothesis and proposed the theory of wave mechanics. It was Schrödinger's proposal that an electron's orbit has to correspond to a wave with a whole number of crests and troughs; that is, it has to be made of a whole wave, or of two waves, or of hundreds of waves, but no fractions of waves are permitted. And further, the theory explained why the orbiting electrons do not gradually radiate energy and spiral into the nucleus. The waves are *standing waves*, analogs of the vibrations of the strings of a violin. A violin string vibrates up and down; crests and troughs do not shift from one end of the instrument to the other. It was implied that an electron *surrounded*, rather than orbited the nucleus and since it had no circular motion, there was no necessity for constantly radiating energy. The interpretation of Schrödinger's waves was subsequently made by German physicist Max Born, who showed that they were a measure of the probability that the electron occupied any specific position. The probability-wave interpretation permitted the combination of the wave and particle descriptions of the electron. The electron was pictured as a wave pattern, the knowledge of which allowed for the determination of the probability that the electron as a particle could be found in a given location.[2]

The problem that still remained was the nature of the electrons that were presumed to be in the nucleus. German physicist Werner Heisenberg had published in 1927 a paper on a fundamental principle of quantum mechanics that he called the "uncertainty principle." It stated that the position and momentum of a quantum particle can never be simultaneously determined. More precisely, if the uncertainty in a particle's position is multiplied by the uncertainty in its momentum the results will be approximately equal to a certain small value called Planck's constant. What this says is that if the position of the particle is determined with more precision, the momentum of the particle must be known with correspondingly reduced precision. The better one quantity is known, the less can be known about the other. It was this restriction that raised serious doubts about nuclear electrons.

The argument was based upon the fact that nuclei are very small, and if an electron were confined to the nucleus, its location would be very precisely defined. This would require that there be a very large uncertainty in its momentum and therefore also in its velocity. The electron might be expected to spend a considerable part of its time moving at high velocity, and this would lead to a considerable nuclear instability.

The problem was solved in 1932 by the English physicist James Chadwick, who discovered a third fundamental particle, the neutron. The neutron had a mass slightly greater than the proton, but carried no charge. Heisenberg was quick to postulate that nuclei consisted of protons and neutrons. The Helium nucleus for example, with a mass four times that of hydrogen, contained two protons and two neutrons and had a +2 charge exactly balancing the -2 charge of its extranuclear electrons. The discovery of the neutron also helped confirm the existence of another particle, the neutrino. German physicist Wolfgang Pauli had first postulated the neutrino as an explanation for the energy loss that occurred in processes where radioactive nuclei disintegrated with the production of beta particles. Now it was possible to explain the origin of the neutrino in the decay of a neutron into a proton, an electron, and a neutrino. Many other particles have since been described, but the neutrino still remains the most elusive. It has no charge or mass, and travels at the speed of light. It may also be the most common particle in the universe—a billion for every proton or electron. But neutrinos rarely react with other matter, and it was only in 1956 that American physicists Clyde Cowan and Frederick Reines detected neutrinos in high-energy particle accelerator experiments.

Shortly after the neutron was discovered, another American physicist, Carl Anderson, discovered a positively charged electron, the positron, in cosmic rays. This was the first demonstration of an "antiparticle," the exact duplicate of the particle but with the opposite charge. Today we know that all subatomic particles come in pairs, though they are rarely detected in nature, but demonstrable in high-energy particle accelerators.

II. Fields of Force

By 1935, there was still a relatively simple picture of subatomic particles. There were only five of them, and three—the proton, the neutron, and the electron—were the only ones making up atoms. Neutrinos were presumably only created in beta decay processes, and positrons were seen only in cosmic rays. But the preceding decade had witnessed another focus of thought for great theorists like Pauli, Heisenberg, and Dirac. It was realized that both subatomic particles and energy quanta could in some cases best be described as fields of force, with subatomic events portrayed as interactions among various types of fields.[3] Admittedly, the descriptions based upon field interactions were in mathematical terms, and a visual counterpart was often difficult to arrive at, but there were nagging problems crying for explanation. For one thing, physicists wondered why the electrical repulsion of the protons in the nucleus did not cause atoms to fly apart. Theorists judged that a force to hold the nucleus together must be perhaps a hundred times the magnitude of the electromagnetic force, so they called it the "strong force" or the "strong nuclear force." The disintegration of the nucleus that occurred with radioactivity was judged to be mediated by a different and very much weaker nuclear force, which was named the "weak force." Together with electromagnetism and gravity, these forces are now thought to be the basic forces of the universe. But the strong and weak nuclear forces are distinguished by the fact that they are felt over only extremely short distances

As quantum field theorists examined the behavior of these forces, they began to realize the full implications of Heisenberg's uncertainty principle. Not only is the principle applicable to the velocity and momentum of an electron, but to any pair of what are called conjugate variables; any pair of variables that are related in a certain reciprocal way. Energy and time are conjugate variables, which means that the energy of a particle cannot be precisely defined over extremely short time periods. In fact, if the time span is short enough, the uncertainty in the energy may be great enough to create new particles out of nothing. These particles are called virtual particles, and their existence is transient indeed.

As Morris describes them: "They spring into existence for tiny fractions of a second, deriving the energy required for their existence from Heisenberg uncertainties. Naturally, they cannot exist for long, for this energy debt soon has to be paid back. When it is, the virtual particles disappear into nothingness again."[4]

It should be stressed that the virtual particle is not viewed as any less *real* during its brief existence, than electrons or protons or neutrons, though the latter are often referred to as *real* particles. Quantum field theorists explain that virtual particles are constantly coming into existence everywhere, even in the empty space of a perfect vacuum. Thus, in quantum theory, the term *nothing* has no meaning. These implications of quantum theory appalled many scientists. As Robert Crease and Charles Mann describe it:

> The Uncertainty Principle exposed a frightful chaos in the lowest order of matter. The spaces around and within atoms, previously thought to be empty, were now supposed to be filled with a boiling soup of ghostly particles. Small wonder that many theorists, including Einstein, were appalled. From the perspective of quantum field theory, the vacuum contains random eddies in the field of space-time: tidal whirlpools that occasionally hurl up bits of matter only to suck them down again. Since these bits virtually don't exist, they have been named "virtual particles."[5]

But these authors go on to point out that virtual particles are far from a bizarre anomaly. In fact, they are a key feature of quantum field theory. Heisenburg, Pauli, and others saw that electromagnetism, the force responsible for light, electricity, and magnetism, can be mediated by the transfer of photons between charged particles. More recently, quantum field theorists have elaborated this concept in a theory called "quantum electrodynamics." The theory proposes that electrons can spontaneously emit virtual photons, and that these photons can be absorbed by other charged particles; the exchange of virtual photons gives rise to the electromagnetic field. The way in which these forces act may be illustrated by means of the analogy of two skaters throwing a ball back and forth. As the ball is exchanged, each skater is forced backwards, as though a force of repulsion existed between them. Alternatively, if the skaters now turned their backs to one another, and threw a boomerang back and forth, the changing direction of the boomerang would force them toward each other. This would be analogous to the force of attraction between a negatively and a positively charged particle. Like all analogies this one fails in that it implies too much about our knowledge of the path followed by the photon, since this is part of the uncertainty that is always present with quantum particles.

Another uncertainty raised by the quantum electrodynamics formulation is much more significant and stems from the fact that the theory predicts certain infinities. For example, when the energy of interaction between an electron and the cloud of virtual particles surrounding it is computed, the result is infinity. In addition, the energy of "empty" space is predicted to be infinite. That is, the energy associated with the appearance of a virtual particle, in the absence of matter, is infinite. Theorists generally see such infinities as signals that something is wrong. However, German physicist Victor Weisskopf suggested a mathematical trick called *renormalization*, in which certain infinite quantities were subtracted from each other to give finite results. Many scientists objected, including Dirac who pointed out that a sensible mathematical approach is to neglect a quantity when it is small, but not when it is infinite. Critics also point out that if we take the results of renormalized quantum electrodynamics (QED) literally, it fails to give us an understandable picture of the nature of subatomic reality. For example, the properties of the electron appear to include infinite mass, infinite charge, and infinite energy. It has been suggested that one possible reason these properties are not actually seen is that the electron is screened by a cloud of virtual particles. In this way the infinite energy of the "bare" electron may be canceled out by the infinite energy of the virtual particle cloud. It may be that QED is telling us that an electron cannot be defined apart from the field that surrounds it.

Once the virtual photon was established as the intermediary in the force of electromagnetism, scientists began to look at the other forces. In 1935 the Japanese physicist Hideki Yukawa postulated a new particle, the meson, which was associated with the strong force in the nucleus. In this case the force between protons and neutrons would be mediated by virtual mesons, just as the electromagnetic force was mediated by virtual photons.

The predicted particle was discovered in 1947 and was called the pi-meson or simply the pion. It had a mass two hundred times that of the electron. It also came in three varieties, with positive, negative, or zero charge. And its spin was zero. Spin was a characteristic of subatomic particles that was first demonstrated for the electron by the Dutch physicists George Uhlenbeck and Samuel Goudsmit in 1925. What they observed was that when light-emitting atoms were placed in a magnetic field, single spectral lines that would indicate the various energy levels of the electrons in the atom were split into two lines, or three lines, or more. They hypothesized that these multiple lines were the result of the interaction of the applied external magnetic field with the electrons that, because of their spin, were acting as tiny magnets. Depending upon the direction in which an electron was spinning, its energy would be increased or decreased. Since different wavelengths of light correspond to different energy transitions, the spectral lines would split.

The zero spin that was observed in the case of the pion placed it in the category of particles that are involved with a force. Such particles are called bosons, and they have either zero spin, or one quantum of spin, or two. Bosons are named after the Indian physicist Satyendra Bose. Another class of particles, called fermions—after Italian physicist Enrico Fermi—have half-integral spin and are particles associated with matter. It should be noted that the designations of integral spin for bosons and half-integral spin for fermions is merely a convention—it does not imply that any particle has "half of a spin." The way in which pions bind protons and neutrons together in the nucleus involves a kind of metamorphosis of particles. Either the proton or the neutron may emit an uncharged pion, which is then absorbed by the other particle. Alternatively, a proton may emit a positively charged pion and become a neutron, and the positively charged pion will then react with a neutron to transform it into a proton. In a third possibility, emission of a negative pion can cause the interchange of proton and neutron. This apparent equivalency of proton and neutron has led physicists to refer to them as *nucleons*.

III. Multiplicity of Particles and a New Kind of Complexity

Since the late 1940s the number of new kinds of particles has multiplied incredibly. Further studies of cosmic-ray showers and experiments with cyclotrons yielded a variety of mesons and a large number of heavier particles that were similar to the proton and neutron. The latter are now referred to as *baryons*. By the end of the 1950s, so many particles had been discovered that the term *elementary particle* was clearly inappropriate. There were hundreds of different mesons, and hundreds of different baryons. And there was no visible limit to the number of particles that might be found in the future. Crease and Mann tell us that by 1958 there were so many new particles that scientists at the University of California at Berkeley began to publish an almanac. The first edition was 19 pages long and discussed sixteen new particles. The edition of 1984 ran 304 pages and referred to two hundred particles.[6]

The field of particle physics was overwhelmed by complexity. The expectation that matter was made up of a few elementary particles had not been realized. Perhaps simplicity was not a realistic expectation, though Morris reminds us that it has been a useful prejudice for science in the past. The Copernican shift to a sun-centered solar system was a move to simplicity. Likewise Newton's inverse square law of gravitation worked for all types of moving bodies—both celestial and terrestrial. Einstein's theory of special relativity simplifies the propagation of light, excluding the need to postulate an ether and to invent complicated mechanisms for light's passage through it. Not all successful physical theories have proved to be simplifications, but the idea seems well founded. And it is often possible to make a distinction between complex phenomena and complex principles. As Morris says, "It would not be inaccurate to define science as the attempt to discover the fundamental simplicity that is hidden behind the apparent complexity of natural phenomena."[7]

A major step in the direction of simplification was desperately needed in the physics of quantum particles, and it was partially achieved by the classification of particles according to the forces that they experienced, particularly the strong and weak nuclear forces. Particles that were affected by the strong force were called hadrons, and included both baryons—heavy particles like the proton and neutron—and mesons. Particles that felt only the weak force were called leptons. The lepton family was made up of the electron, the muon (a particle found in cosmic rays and originally confused with the pion) and the neutrino. Since the classification scheme was developed, several more particles have been added to the lepton group. One is called the tuon, and two more resulted from the observation that the neutrino occurs in two additional forms.

This classification brought some relief to particle physicists, though it still left the hadron category far too large. A second step for subdivision of the hadron group was proposed in 1961 by American physicist Murray Gell-Mann and Israeli physicist Yuval Ne'eman. It allowed for the most commonly observed baryons and mesons to be put together in sets of eight and was called, somewhat facetiously, the eightfold way. The original eightfold way was a path to enlightenment devised by the Buddha in the fifth or sixth century BC. The proposal was made that hadrons were separable into groups by virtue of the presence of different subatomic consistuents. Gell-Mann called these components quarks. Originally there were three of these: up, down, and strange, and each had an antiparticle. All particles have antiparticles. The positron, a positive electron, which was discussed in connection with the early discoveries of particle physics, is an example of an antiparticle. According to the theory, which was elaborated by Gell-Mann and independently by American physicist George Zweig, all the hundreds of baryons and mesons could be explained as combinations of six types of quarks and antiquarks. Baryons were made up of three quarks, mesons of a quark and an antiquark. The proton, for example, contained one down and two up quarks, while the positively charged pion would have an up and an antidown quark. The large number of particles in the baryon and meson categories can be explained by this scheme with the added qualification that energy changes lead to slightly different particles. Many of the new particles were nothing more than higher-energy states of the old particles.

The existence of quarks was verified in 1968 in an experiment performed with the Stanford Linear Accelerator. However, this relatively simplified quark theory was short-lived. From 1974 to 1984, three more quarks were found to be necessary to explain newly discovered hadrons, and, in addition, all six quarks appeared to carry an additional characteristic called *color*. They could be either red or green or blue. The color designations did not imply actual color—quarks are too small to be involved in light interactions—but were simply three additional charge-related properties that were part of the character of quarks. The upshot of this refinement was that there were now eighteen different quarks. Quarks came in six *flavors*, as they were called: up, down, strange, charmed, bottom, and top; and three different colors: red, green, and blue.[8]

Some additional insight into the way quarks may function was provided by a theory proposed in the mid-1970s called quantum chromodynamics. This theory is analogous to quantum electrodynamics (QED), the theory that we discussed earlier in connection with the interaction of particles with electromagnetic fields by means of virtual photons. In quantum chromodynamics (QCD), quark color is viewed as analogous to electrical charge. Color "charges" bind quarks together in hadrons in the way electrical charges bind electrons and nuclei together in atoms. QCD is viewed as a successful theory because it explains the forces that bind quarks in hadrons, and it also provides further insight into how mesons provide for the force between protons and neutrons. Since mesons contain quarks, it is really the interaction between quarks that joins protons and neutrons. But

QCD brings one more complexity. In QED there are only two kinds of charge, positive and negative. The interactions are mediated by one virtual particle, the photon. In QCD there are at least three color charges (and perhaps their anticolor as well), and the theory calls for eight different entities called *gluons*, the analogs of the virtual photon in QED. The interaction between particles, such as an electron or a quark leads to the emission of a gluon; the recoil from this emission changes the velocity of the particle. The gluon then collides with another matter particle and is absorbed. This collision changes the velocity of the second particle, just as though there had been a force between the two matter particles.

But the search for simpler explanations for the multiplicity of subatomic particles in terms of the forces they experienced seems to have led us to even greater complexity. It has opened up whole new areas for theoretical and experimental work. And the experimental component has been left far behind! As Morris expresses it:

> QCD is quite an elegant theory, but it does not have the simplicity that the physicists who proposed the original version of the quark theory were seeking. Three quarks have not proved to be adequate to explain observed phenomena. Six different quark flavors are now known. According to QCD, each of these six quarks can have any of three different colors. Thus the number of different kinds of quark has been multiplied to eighteen (or thirty-six, if antiquarks are counted separately). In addition, there are eight gluons, making twenty-six particles in all…. It appears that the search for simplicity has only led to a new kind of complexity. Perhaps quarks are not really the fundamental constituents of matter. There is no reason why quarks could not be made of yet smaller particles. If they are, the same might be true of leptons.[9]

Morris goes on to say that quarks and leptons may be the ultimate constituents of matter. On the other hand, there may be additional levels, and even the possibility that there are an infinite number of levels. Quarks and leptons may be composed of smaller particles, which are composed of yet smaller particles, and so on. Morris concludes: "Physical reality could conceivably be a kind of cosmic onion, with level below level below level. It may be that the levels never come to an end."[10]

IV. The New View of Physical Reality

This review of the history and recent advances in subatomic physics should serve to convince the reader that matter is not at all what we thought it was just a decade or two ago. There is indeed what appears to be a fascinating kind of chaos at the lowest order of matter; virtual particles boiling up out of nothing and electrons that appear to possess infinite mass and energy.

Then, too, hadrons like protons and neutrons appear to be made up of a grand variety of subunits called quarks, and perhaps the lepton family—including electrons—also possess subunit structure. All these new developments are heavily laced with the hypothetical, a trend that seems more and more prevalent as the difficulty of experimental verification increases. It seems more and more the case that the empirical support for our mathematical models is less accessible, as though physical reality is a shadow receding from our view.

We wonder if it is not time for a look at a broader framework for meaning, for a reality only hinted at by our science but that may be profoundly deeper and infinitely larger than that which our finite minds can ever hope to fully embrace?

In the progression of hierarchies, theology seems better positioned, with its highly integrative character, to suggest an approach to that deeper reality. Yet, it too works only with models and metaphors of reality, and so even at this level of integration—mankind, nature, and God—we are faced with the limitations of our own minds and the narrowness of our cultural experience and see only dimly the vast unseen and its Creator who lies behind, yet may be the One "in whom we live and move and have our being."

Summary

Our goal in this chapter has been to examine in some detail the experimental data of the physics of subatomic particles in order to assess the current status of matter as a candidate for physical reality. At each new milestone of discovery in the century-old study we are confronted by ever-increasing complexity and multiplied mystery. Our scientific models are challenged to embrace such phenomena as quantum uncertainty and subatomic interactions mediated by a seeming chaos of "boiling" virtual particles. And as we go deeper into the mysteries of matter, the opportunities for experimental verification of our models require ever more powerful tools and so become more and more difficult to achieve.

Physical reality seems less and less tangible. Perhaps in the end it may only serve to point us to another awe-inspiring transcendent and immanent Reality.

3

Reality as Unity of the Forces of Nature

I. The First Unification

In *The Critique of Pure Reason*, philosopher Immanuel Kant argued that all human wisdom is limited because our minds must impose a structure on our experience. The consequence of this, in the words of Robert Crease and Charles Mann, is as follows:

> As a consequence, we are led inevitably to make certain suppositions about nature that are, in actuality, by-products of the organizing activity of our own brains. Such presuppositions—Kant showed their number, and said they apply to more than science—are unprovable in theory but indispensable in practice. He called them "regulative ideas," and listed the unity of nature as a cardinal example. Because of it, the structure of science itself draws physicists toward unification.[1]

Recall that in chapter 1 we mentioned that Albert Einstein had expressed a deep passion to know the mind of God, to know nature as to intent and purpose. Indeed, the search for a unified field theory occupied the greatest part of his later scientific life. For Einstein there was a remarkable harmony between the human mind and the rationality embedded in the universe, and he sought the explanation for that harmony in the unification of the four forces of nature—the strong and the weak nuclear forces, the electromagnetic force and gravity.

The beginnings of unification go back to the Scottish physicist and mathematician, James Clerk Maxwell, who built a theory of the electromagnetic field on the experimental work of English scientist Michael Faraday. Timothy Ferris, in his *Coming of Age in the Milky Way*, tells us that the Edison-like Faraday was a prodigious experimenter, who in the course of forty-six years of research on electricity and magnetism at the prestigious Royal Institution of Great Britain performed more than fifteen thousand experiments.[2] His great contribution was to bring about a fundamental shift in emphasis from the apparatus of electricity, the magnets and coils, to the invisible fields of force that surrounded them.

However, it was Maxwell who provided the deep insights and mathematical skills necessary to build a quantitative structure, and to show that electricity and magnetism were aspects of a single force, electromagnetism, and that even light was an expression of this force. This field theory was so unique, so counter to the current preference for mechanical models, that Maxwell felt obliged to invent a mechanical description just for Faraday's benefit. And there was another doubter of equal prestige, Sir William Thompson (Lord Kelvin), who found Maxwell's equations so disturbing that he stated that in departing from mechanical models Maxwell had lapsed into mysticism.

This was an interesting charge, since Maxwell was a fervent evangelical Christian who claimed that he approached his science with the openness of one who expected that God's Creation would be rightly studied with an all-important metaphysical reference to the vastness of nature and narrowness of our symbolic sciences.[3]

As Thomas Torrance says of Maxwell in *A Dynamical Theory of the Electromagnetic Field*:

> No human science, he felt, could ever really match up in its theoretical connections to the real modes of connection existing in nature, for valid as they may be in mathematical and symbolic systems, they were true only up to a point and could only be accepted by men of science, as well as by men of faith, in so far as they were allowed to point human scientific inquiry beyond its own limits to that hidden region where thought weds fact, and where the mental operation of the mathematician and the physical action of nature are seen in their true relation. That is to say, as Clerk Maxwell himself understood it, physical science cannot be rightly pursued without taking into account an all-important metaphysical reference to the ultimate ground of nature's origin in the Creator. Thus while Clerk Maxwell never intruded his theological and deeply evangelical convictions into his physical and theoretical science, he clearly allowed his Christian belief in God the Creator and Sustainer of the universe to exercise some regulative control in his judgment as to the appropriateness and tenability of his scientific theories, that is, as to whether they measured up as far as possible to "the riches of creation."[4]

Could we have, in Maxwell's attitude, another of Kant's regulative ideas? Could the "riches of creation" be another presupposition like the unity of nature? And was it perhaps the more indispensable of the two for James Maxwell? The same question could be asked for another deeply religious scientist, Albert Einstein, who almost single-handedly brought about a revolution in physics in this century. In the theory of special relativity he showed that mass and energy were equivalent, and in the theory of general relativity he showed that space and time were one inseparable space-time continuum.

But he was not to be successful in his quest for a unified field theory.

II. Problems with Further Unification

By the last quarter of this century our understanding of the array of particles and forces and their relationships came to be known as the standard model. As discussed in the last chapter, the model includes two general categories of particles. Those of fractional spin (one-half) are called fermions, and those of integral spin (zero, one, or two) are called bosons. Fermions comprise matter, and obey the Pauli exclusion principle, which excludes the possibility that any two fermions can occupy a given quantum state at the same time. For this reason only a limited number of electrons can occupy each energy shell in a given atom. Protons, neutrons, and electrons are fermions. Protons and neutrons are made up of quarks—three quarks per nucleon. Bosons convey force, and function as exchange particles between fermions. They do not obey the exclusion principle, so several different forces may be acting simultaneously.

The standard model is completed by the inclusion of the four fundamental forces—electromagnetism, gravitation, and the strong and weak nuclear forces. The boson for electromagnetism is the photon; that for the weak forces in called a weak boson; that for the strong force is called a gluon, and for gravitation the graviton.

In principle, every fundamental event in the universe in explainable by the standard model, yet, as Timothy Ferris tells us in *Coming of Age in the Milky Way*, it is hardly considered the last word by physicists.[5] Ferris quotes physicist Leon Lederman, director of the Fermilab particle accelerator in a 1965 interview:

> The trouble we're in now is that the standard model is very elegant, it's very powerful, it explains so much—but it's not complete. It has some flaws, and one of its greatest flaws is aesthetic. It's too complicated. It has too many arbitrary parameters. We don't really see the creator twiddling seventeen knobs to set seventeen parameters to create the universe as we know it. The picture is not beautiful, and that drive for beauty and simplicity and symmetry has been an unfailing guidepost to how to go in physics.[6]

Then Ferris concludes:

> So it was that physicists late in the century were still searching for a simpler and more efficient account of the fundamental interactions. The object of their quest went by the name "unified" theory, by which they usually meant a single theory that would account for two or more of the forces currently handled by separate theories. They were guided, to be sure, by experimental data and by the challenges immediately at hand—the theorist resembles, as Einstein said, an "unscrupulous opportunist," more often trying to find a specific solution to an immediate problem than to write a grand explication of everything. But they were guided as well, as Lederman mentions, by the hope that their accounts of nature could more nearly approach the elegant simplicity and superlative creativity of nature herself.[7]

III. Symmetry as the Clue to Unification

Given the limitations mentioned by Lederman and the general problems with particle physics discussed in the previous chapter, physicists were clearly in need of some more fundamental understanding if a unified theory was ever to be realized. At this juncture the most promising clue was symmetry. Ferris opens up this topic with a beautiful and artistic description of the symmetries of nature.[8] In each instance symmetry is found to be definable in part as the repetition of a measurable quantity. To this definition the Greeks added the qualification "due proportion," meaning that the repetition should also be harmonious and aesthetically pleasing. In science the definition could be simply: symmetry exists when a measurable quantity remains invariant or unchanged under a transformation or alteration. In fact, all the laws of nature are expressions of invariances and may therefore involve symmetries. And the principle had proved extensively useful in the past, with the revelation of previously unknown laws by looking for symmetrical relationships in nature. Einstein's theory of special relativity employed the Lorenz transformations to maintain the invariance of Maxwell's field equations for observers in motion. And in the general theory of relativity he did a similar thing for observers in strong gravitational fields.

When this principle was applied to the quantum physics of particles and fields, it opened up an extremely promising approach to unified field theory. We should first note that a familiar symmetry is the identity of all subatomic particles of a given variety; all protons are identical, for example. Another symmetry is the identity of fields of force with the same quantum numbers; all electromagnetic fields are identical. This, in a much simplified form, is the concept behind unified field theory. The approach had early successes in the classification of subatomic particles into symmetry groups by Eugene Wigner and in the prediction of the existence of anti-matter in the form of the positron by Paul Dirac.

However, its function in the search for unknown fields awaited the development of what is called gauge field theory. The foundation for gauge field theory was laid by Einstein's friend Hermann Weyl in 1918, when he attempted to show that electromagnetism, like gravity, is linked to a symmetry of space, a step toward showing that the two forces are aspects of the same thing.[9] In his proposal, Weyl talked about "gauge symmetries," and specified that they occurred in two varieties, local and global. Though the idea of local and global gauge symmetries or invariances is difficult to visualize, the key concept is that if any physical system is to demonstrate local symmetry or invariance there must exist one aspect that precisely compensates for changes in another aspect to preserve the invariance. The logical explanation for the compensation is the action of a force, presumably mediated by force particles or bosons. Crease and Mann propose the following example from the world of economics:

> [An] example of global symmetry can be drawn from the world of high finance, or at least that portion of it described in elementary economics textbooks. If the income of every person and the price of every commodity suddenly increased tenfold, nothing would happen. People would still spend their wages on the same things in the same way, except that now paychecks and prices would have an extra zero. The supply and demand of every commodity would be undisturbed and, in the jargon of economists, all markets would still "clear." The forces of supply and demand can be said to be globally symmetric with respect to a change in the economic measuring stick—money.

> Now imagine that incomes and prices were to jump around *randomly*, some rising, some falling by different chance amounts. The situation should then change dramatically: Supply and demand would be out of whack. Some people would be clamoring to buy more than is currently offered for sale, while others would be unable to afford their previous standard of living. This state of affairs, according to classical economists, brings into play the "invisible hand" of market forces. Prices adjust, decreasing in one place, increasing in another, until once again all markets clear. Automatically compensating for each random change in the system, the invisible hand maintains the original symmetry, which in this case is a *local* one. (In fact, economists make such claims only for small stochastic perturbations, but the principle holds true.)

> Given the arbitrariness of the changes in local symmetry, it is hard to believe that any physical system could have this property. And indeed, gauge symmetries cannot occur unless the random changes in one aspect of a system are precisely compensated for by a change in another aspect, so that a quantity related to both remains conserved. Such compensation

cannot take place unless a force intervenes. Indeed, it presupposes the existence of one. Maintaining local gauge invariance is not an easy, passive task; the Universe must act to preserve it. Thus understanding a force means tracing it back to an originating symmetry.[10]

Ferris tells us that the first gauge field theory beyond the electromagnetic theory was invented by Yang Chen Ning and Robert Mills in 1954. Yang had been fascinated by the gauge invariance of the electromagnetic field. Its implicit symmetry enabled Einstein to deduce that the velocity of light was the same for all observers, regardless of position or motion. Yang hoped to describe a similar invariance for the strong force, noting that the strong force treats protons and neutrons identically, despite the fact that one is charged and the other not. We could say, then, that the strong force is invariant under transformations of electric charge. Yang failed to write a suitably symmetrical equation for the strong force, but in the course of his efforts the idea of force as the agency that connects local invariances to universal laws was clearly articulated. The paper that Yang and Mills eventually published on gauge field theory offered an entirely new approach to theoretical physicists. As Ferris describes it:

> What one could now do was to first identify an invariance, the signal of a symmetry; then construct, mathematically, a gauge field capable of maintaining that invariance locally; then derive the characteristics of the particles that would convey such a field; then go and see (or urge the experimenters to go see) whether any such particles actually exist in nature. Viewed from this perspective, Einstein's photons, the carriers of the electromagnetic force, are gauge particles, messengers of symmetry. So are the gravitons thought to be the carriers of gravitation.[11]

IV. Symmetry and Broken Symmetry

While symmetry was to continue to be an important concept in the development of quantum field theory, a number of investigations had revealed that asymmetries also exist in nature. In fact, it was Yang and another colleague, Lee Tsung-Dao who had identified a discrete asymmetry in the weak force that was called parity violation; particles emitted by beta decay events showed a slight preference for spin in one direction rather than the other. In other words, the weak force does not function symmetrically with respect to spin. Subsequently, experiments performed by physicist Chien-Shiung Wu confirmed the Yang and Lee prediction. The question of why nature was sometimes symmetrical and at other times asymmetric was intriguing and significant in the minds of a number of physicists. Among those investigating asymmetries was Steven Weinberg, who along with Abdus Salam and Sheldon Glashow made the next step in the approach to unified field theory. Weinberg was especially interested in how asymmetrical relationships develop from symmetrical natural laws. Ferris gives an example of how such relationships may have originated.[12] If a handful of sharpened pencils is gathered into a tight cylindrical bundle, balanced on their points, and then released, there is a moment during which they remain rotationally symmetrical. But the symmetry is unstable, and in an instant the pencils will fall into an unsymmetrical jumble like the onset of a game of pickup sticks. In the simile, the jumble of fallen pencils is the universe today, and the neat bundle at the start is the symmetric form in which the universe was thought to have begun. Physics, in seeking a unified field theory, is looking for the deeper symmetry hidden beneath the extant broken symmetry.

Weinberg, Salam, and Glashow had each struggled for a common denominator between two of the four forces, electromagnetism and the weak nuclear force. Glashow had published in 1961 about the remarkable similarities between the two, and predicted the existence of what were called W and Z force-carrying particles, but he was unable to predict their masses. Then it was demonstrated by several workers that symmetry-breaking events could create new kinds of force-carrying particles, some of which could be massive. It was then reasoned that if the particles that carry the weak nuclear and electromagnetic forces were related by a broken symmetry, it must be possible to determine experimentally the masses of the W and Z particles characteristic of the unified, symmetrical force from which the two forces may have arisen. Weinberg had been using the symmetry-breaking ideas, but applying them to the strong force. All at once, in 1967, he realized that the particle descriptions coming from his equations—one set massless, the other massive—did not resemble the strong force, but fit perfectly the expectations of the electromagnetic and the weak forces. The massless particle was the photon of the electromagnetic force. The massive particles were the Ws and Zs implicated in the weak nuclear force.

The test of the theory required a particle accelerator of tremendous power, and the two leading candidates were at CERN, the European Center for Nuclear Research, near Geneva, and Fermilab, located in a western suburb of Chicago. Ferris's comparison of the two facilities is instructive.[13] Fermilab had been built under the direction of Robert Wilson, who was not only a physicist but also an architect and sculptor. The entrance to the facility was marked by a Wilson sculpture, a looming construction of steel arches with the title, *Broken Symmetry*. The accelerator tunnel, buried beneath the Illinois plain, was delineated by an earthwork berm within which buffalo grazed. The administration building was a sweeping convex tower that Wilson had modeled on the proportion of the Beauvais Cathedral in France. His intent in this design was based upon several related ideas. In Philip Hilts's *Scientific Temperaments* he is quoted as having said: "I found a striking similarity between the tight community of cathedral builders and community of accelerator builders. Both of them were daring innovators, both were fiercely competitive on national lines, but yet both were basically internationalists....They recognized themselves as technically oriented; one of their slogans was *Ars sine scientia nihil est!*—art without science is nothing." [14]

Ferris's description of the CERN facility is less enthusiastic:

> CERN, for its part, looked about as aesthetically unified as a Bolshevik boiler factory. Its administration building, slapped together from prefabricated plastic panels and aluminum alloy window frames that bled pepper-gray corrosives in the rain, called to mind less Beauvais Cathedral than the public housing projects of suburban Gorky. Its laboratories were scattered across the landscape, as haphazardly as the debris from a trucking accident, on a plot of land that straddled the French-Swiss border outside of Geneva. The prevailing style was late Tower of Babel, with scientists switching from French to German to English in mid-sentence while lunching at the laboratory cafeterias, one of which accepted only French currency and the other only Swiss. Yet for all its air of disorder, CERN worked every bit as well as Fermilab, and by the early 1970s was beginning to surpass it. [15]

Indeed, it was a CERN accelerator group that eventually found the W and Z bosons. Its leader, Carlo Rubbia, announced in early 1963 that the W particle had been found and the electroweak theory thus confirmed. Shortly thereafter they found the predicted Z boson as well. Thus Weinberg, Salam, and Glashow had been proved correct. We do indeed appear to live in a universe of broken symmetries, where at least two of the fundamental forces, electromagnetism and the weak nuclear force, have diverged from a single, more symmetrical parent. Stephen Hawking, in his book *A Brief History of Time*, provides another useful perspective on the Weinberg-Salam theory. [16] What appear to be several completely different force particles at low energies are actually all the same type of particle, but in different states. At high energies all the particles behave the same. At some intermediate energy, what he calls "spontaneous symmetry breaking" occurs, and the particles of the electroweak force differentiate into those of the individual electromagnetic and weak nuclear forces. To illustrate, Hawking provides an analogy from the gambling casino:

> The effect is rather like the behavior of a roulette ball on a roulette wheel. At high energies (when the wheel is spun quickly) the ball behaves in essentially only one way—it rolls round and round. But as the wheel slows,

the energy of the ball decreases, and eventually the ball drops into one of the thirty-seven slots in the wheel. In other words, at low energies there are thirty-seven different states in which the ball can exist. If, for some reason, we could only observe the ball at low energies, we would then think that there were thirty-seven different types of ball![17]

Still to be explained is how symmetry breaking leads to the acquisition of mass by the W and Z bosons, though Weinberg has postulated a new particle, the Higgs boson, as the symmetry breaking agent.

Further unification has been attempted by theorists who have sought to join the electroweak theory with the strong nuclear force in a series of proposals referred to as the grand unified theories (GUTs). The first of these was published by Glashow and his American physicist colleague Howard Georgi. As Hawking points out, the title grand unified theory was a bit of an exaggeration: "The resultant theories are not all that grand, nor are they fully unified, as they do not include gravity."[18] The basic concept of the GUTs is that the strong nuclear force gets weaker at high energies, whereas the electromagnetic and weak nuclear forces get stronger at high energies. Therefore, at some very high energy, called the grand unification energy, these three forces would all have the same strengths and so could be just different aspects of a single force. The grand unification energy would have to be much more than a million times larger than any particle accelerator can achieve. In fact, the accelerator would need to be the size of the solar system! It is therefore impossible to test grand unified theories directly in the laboratory.

However, there are low-energy consequences that are potentially testable. The most interesting and controversial consequence is that the theory predicts the instability of protons. As Hawking explains it, at the grand unification energy there is no difference between a quark and a positron. The three quarks that make up a proton normally do not have the energy to change into a positron, but "very occasionally, one of them may acquire sufficient energy to make the transition because the uncertainty principle means that the energy of the quarks inside the proton cannot be fixed exactly. The proton would then decay."[19]

The probability of this occurrence is extremely small but the chances are improved greatly if one is observing a large quantity of matter. One experiment has involved the study of eight thousand tons of water stored in a salt mine in Ohio (to limit cosmic-ray interference). Thus far no proton decay has been observed, despite the fact that theoretically there has been adequate time for the event to occur. The instability of the proton, if it is successfully demonstrated, would open the way for an important additional predictive success for the GUTs. For these theories postulate the existence of new particles (called x) that are bosons that have the property of turning quarks into leptons, or leptons into quarks. At the high energies of the early universe, real x particles could have been formed and would have led to the excess of matter over antimatter that we have now. All that would be necessary was an unequal production of particles and antiparticles in the lepton-quark interchange.

Critics of the GUTs, like American physicist Julian Schwinger, Glashow's mentor, caution that the unification theory has gone far beyond experiment. He says:

> Unification is the ultimate goal of science, it's true. But that it should be unification now—surely that's the original definition of hubris. There are a heck of a lot of energies we haven't gotten to yet. Grand unified schemes make the implicit assumption that what happens in them is not fundamentally different from what we know—an assumption about how nature works that's in conflict with what we've spent the last century learning.[20]

In fact, the GUTs have not proved successful in linking the electroweak and strong nuclear forces, but, as Timothy Ferris expresses it, their "waning...went widely unmourned."[21] They have lacked the "sweeping simplicity" that unified theories are supposed to possess; like the standard model, they were replete with arbitrary parameters, and they omitted the force of gravity. As Freeman Dyson sums it up, "The ground of physics is littered with the corpses of unified theories."[22]

V. Superstring Theory

One still-bright hope for unification is superstring theory, which is built on two very good ideas: (1) the universe has extra, hidden dimensions; (2) subatomic particles are actually not little points but rather little strings. The idea of hidden dimensions was first proposed by the German physicist Theodor Kaluza in 1919. His theory involved the incorporation of electromagnetism into a five-dimensional form of general relativity, and it was later modified by Swedish physicist Oskar Klein to take into account quantum theory. In Klein's version, the fifth dimension was hidden, curled up into a tiny circle and apparently playing no real role in our world. The Kaluza-Klein theory went largely unnoticed until, nearly fifty years later, it was revived in what Crease and Mann call "a strikingly different context, the multidimensional string theories."[23] String theory portrays subatomic particles not as dimensionless points but rather as extended objects that are longer than they are wide and look and behave something like strings. The strings can vibrate, and the rate at which they vibrate can generate the properties of all known particles and an infinite variety of other possible particles as well. Perhaps the most fascinating thing about string theory is that the bewildering diversity of subatomic particles may all be explained as *differing harmonies of the strings.*[24] String theory offered possible answers to some of the most perplexing problems in unification. For example, all of the quantum field theories struggle with perplexing infinities. Recall that quantum electrodynamics, discussed in the last chapter, predicts infinite energies between an electron and the cloud of virtual particles surrounding it. Renormalization, the mathematical manipulation used in these kinds of situations, is strongly criticized by many physicists. The solution from string theory stems from the fact that elementary particles no longer have zero dimension. Zero dimension is a situation that permits exchanges to occur when particles are infinitely close to each other, and the exchange of force infinite. Since strings have length, these are excluded. Another question string theory seems to resolve relates to the curious difference between gravitons, which have spin two, and the other force particles, which have spin one. The answer from string theory is that a string can either by open, meaning it has two ends, or closed, meaning that the ends are joined in a loop. Open strings would be spin-one particles, closed strings spin-two. String theory also requires that gravity be part of the picture, thus providing a means to bring gravity into the quantum field theories, an essential feature of unification. String theory also had its mathematical headaches, but these were largely alleviated by assuming that space-time had more than the usual number of dimensions. Ten or twenty-six or five hundred and six dimensions must be postulated if the theory is to be mathematically correct. Assuming the simplest picture—ten dimensions—the question arises as to how the other six dimensions might be expressed. In the Kaluza-Klein theory, the one extra dimension was folded up into a minute circle. Perhaps the six extra dimensions of string theory could exist in compacted form also—collapsed into structures so tiny that they go unnoticed. Steven Weinberg favored this idea, and the story goes that Howard Georgi, who had worked on the grand unified theory, introduced him at a 1984 Harvard lecture by producing the following limerick:

> Steven Weinberg, returning from Texas
> Brings dimensions galore to perplex us
> But the extra ones all
> Are rolled up in a ball
> So tiny it never affects us.[25]

The fact that "it never affects us" was a source of no little irritation for Georgi and many other physicists who have become very disenchanted with unification theories in general. All of them continue to suffer with the terrible deficiency of intestability by experiment. Weinberg himself voiced the fear that without what he called "that wonderful fertilization that we normally get from experiment," there was danger of drifting into ionospheric reaches of pure abstract thought.[26] For his part, Sheldon Glashow suggested that superstrings theorizing may become an activity "as remote from conventional particle physics as particle physics is from chemistry, to be conducted at schools of divinity by future equivalents of medieval theologians.... For the first time since the Dark Ages, we can see how our noble search may end, with faith replacing science once again."[27]

From our perspective the very future of physics lies in the *faith* of its practitioners that the self-revealing God of the universe will continue to reveal to finite minds some of the meaning behind the infinitely complex universe that he has made. Glashow himself revealed that faith was a part of his science when he talked to Crease and Mann in a 1982 interview. The question was why unification was the necessary outcome of physics. His answer was: "It's not necessary. All I can say is that if you have faith you have an advantage. Physicists in the past who have looked for simplifying, unifying assumptions have done well. Better than physicists who haven't. But there is no *reason* that things get simpler. They could become more and more chaotic and more and more complicated. They may, at some point. But so far things are getting simpler. I can't say simple, but simpler."[28]

We all live by faith!

Ferris points out that the other Greek definition of symmetry, "due proportion," contributes to the invariance aspect that crucial element of aesthetics. Implied in all this is that there is a higher order of perfection that we glimpse through symmetry theories.

One gets the feeling that much, much more lies behind the fascinating world of forces and particles, that a wondrous story will one day be told of what the real universe looks like. Perhaps we look now at only shattered remnants of the perfection of the creation, at the results of broken symmetries.

As Ferris so eloquently says it:

> Supersymmetry portrays this ultimate perfection as a hyperdimensional universe, of which our poor imperfect universe is but a paltry shadow. It implies that physicists—in identifying, say, the weak and electrodynamic forces as having arisen from the breaking of the more symmetrical electroweak force, or in finding concealed symmetries cowering in the cramped nuclear precincts where the strong force does its work—are in effect piecing together the shattered potsherds of that perfect world. Indeed, the theory indicates that there may be countless more such debris, in the form of "shadow matter," supersymmetric particles that have as yet remained undetected because they interact only weakly or not at all with the particles we are made of and have come to know.[29]

But, if we see now only the debris of broken symmetries, then the symmetries that we look for must be part of the past, when the universe was in a state of enormously high energy. So it is that we are driven, for scientific reasons, to questions that formerly were left to theologians. We must search for the *origin* of the universe.

VI. Beginnings

The joining of the fields of particle physics and cosmology brought with it very powerful insights. It was realized that every subatomic particle may have arisen at some point in a process of cosmic evolution. The perplexing array of particles simply attested to the richness of cosmic history. Ferris points out that it is possible to see a direct relationship between the size, binding energy, and age of the fundamental structures of nature.[30] A molecule is larger and more fragile than an atom; atoms are larger and more fragile than nuclei, nuclei are larger but less stable than the quarks of which they are composed. Cosmology tells us that this is a historical relationship. Quarks were first to be bound together in the extremely energetic early moments of the big bang, followed by the union of protons and neutrons to form the nuclei of atoms as expansion and cooling of the universe occurred, and then electrons found their way into relationship with the nuclei to form atoms that in turn joined together to form molecules. The more closely we examine the structures of nature, the farther back we are looking in time. Ferris gives an interesting example:

> Look at something familiar—the back of your hand, let us say—and imagine that you can turn up the magnification to any desired power. At a relatively low magnification you will discern individual cells in the skin, each looming as large and complex as a city, its boundaries delineated by the cell wall. Increase the magnification and you will see, within the cell, a tangle of meandering ribosomes and undulating mitochondria, spherical lysosomes and starburst centrioles—whole neighborhoods full of complex apparatus devoted to the respiratory, sanitary, and energy-producing functions that maintain the cell. Here, already, we encounter ample evidence of history: Though this particular cell is only a few years old, its architecture dates back more than a billion years, to the time when eukaryotic cells like this one first evolved on Earth.
>
> To determine where the cell obtained the blueprint that told it how to form, move into the nucleus and behold the lanky contours of the DNA macromolecules secreted within its genes. Each holds a wealth of genetic information accumulated over the course of some four billion years of evolution. Stored in a nucleotide alphabet of four "letters"—made of sugar and phosphate molecules and replete with punctuation marks, reiterations to guard against error, and superfluities accumulated in blind alleys of

evolutionary history—its message spells out just how to make a human being, from skin and bones to brain cells.

Turn up the magnification some more and you can see that the DNA molecule is composed of many atoms, their outer electron shells intertwined and festooned in a miraculous variety of shapes, from hourglasses to ascending coils like lanky springs to ellipses fat as shields and threads thin as cheroots. Some of these electrons are new arrivals, recently snatched away from neighboring atoms; others joined up with their atomic nuclei more than five billion years ago, in the nebula from which the earth was formed. Increase the magnification a hundred thousand times, and the nucleus of a single carbon atom swells to fill the field of view. Such nuclei were assembled inside a star that exploded long before the sun was born; the age of this one might be anywhere from five to fifteen billion years or more. Finally, looking closer still, one can perceive the trios of quarks that make up each proton and neutron in the nucleus. The quarks have been bound together since the universe was but a few seconds old.[31]

It should be noted, too, that as we have moved back in time we have also moved to higher and higher binding energies. Only a few thousand electron volts of energy are required to strip an atom of its electrons. Several million electron volts are required to split up the nucleons, the protons, and neutrons of the nucleus, but hundreds of times that energy would be required to dislodge the quarks. The fundamental principle is that the smaller, more fundamental structures are bound by the higher energy levels because they were the structures forged in the heat of the big bang.

Current understanding of the events that occurred in the very early universe have been likened by Ferris to climbing a stairway into the past—"a stairway to heaven."[32] He asks us to imagine that we are standing at its base, in the present, in a ten- to twenty-billion-year-old universe. Each step that we take upward takes us back to one-tenth of the age of the universe represented by the previous step. At step one the date is one billion years after the beginning of time (ABT). Our own Milky Way galaxy burns vividly, with a bright, blue-white quasar at its center. The newly forming disk is distorted by clouds of dust and gas, and bisects a spherical halo of bright, first-generation stars. The neighboring Virgo galaxy is much closer now than it will be in our own time when the expansion of the universe will have carried it away to a great distance. The ambient temperature is a chilly three degrees Kelvin (K). At the second step, one hundred million years ABT, there is only darkness. Only a very few stars will have begun to form from the swirling hydrogen and helium gases of this era.

In two more steps, we encounter a blinding light. The time is one million years ABT and photon decoupling has occurred. The cosmic gases have thinned so that photons can travel some distance before their energy is absorbed. It is this light, much red-shifted and diluted because of the expansion of the universe, that will be detected in our own day as the cosmic microwave background radiation. In this same period, energies will fall sufficiently that electrons will be able to unite with nuclei to form hydrogen and helium, and simple organic molecules.

The temperature of the universe is beginning to rise significantly. By step six it has reached ten thousand degrees Kelvin, hotter than the sun's surface. By step eleven, one month ABT the ambient temperature surpasses that at the center of our sun, and at the fifteenth step—five minutes ABT—it reaches one billion degrees Kelvin. At this point, the universe is already cool enough to allow nucleons to join to form atomic nuclei of deuterium and helium. Above this step there are no stable nuclei.

Between the seventeenth and eighteenth steps, at about one second ABT, neutrino decoupling occurs, and a shower of these penetrating particles is released (and still roams the universe today). The universe is denser than rock and as hot as a hydrogen bomb.

Continuing our ascent, at step twenty-two (10^{-6} seconds ABT) we can find no protons or neutrons; only an ocean of free quarks and other elementary particles. We would expect to find that there is a slight excess of quarks over antiquarks, so that when all the annihilation reactions have finished, quarks will be left to form all the matter of the latter-day universe. As we continue, we enter the period of symmetry breaking, when the four forces of the universe are restored to their primeval form. In step twenty-seven (10^{-11} second ABT), the functions of the weak and electromagnetic forces are found to be mediated by a single force, the electroweak. Sufficient energy is present for the creation of the W and Z bosons that mediate electromagnetic and weak nuclear forces interchangeably. Prior to this step, for some unknown period, the universe is ruled by only three forces—gravity, the strong nuclear force, and the electroweak force

The next two dozen steps are clouded in mystery. Some physicists refer to this period as a "desert." Upwards of the fortieth step there may have been a period of very rapid expansion; the universe would have been empty, with all its latent matter and energy swallowed up by the rapidly expanding vacuum. This inflation is postulated to explain the remarkable observation that the universe is poised at an overall mass density that will allow it to expand forever, and also to explain its relative uniformity.

At the sixtieth step, when the universe in only 10^{-43} seconds old, we reach what is called the Planck epoch, and a locked door. It is locked because we do not know what to do about gravitation in a unified theory. If we find that answer, perhaps we will understand the beginning of time. Or perhaps there will be other locked doors. Many physicists believe we will one day know, and it will be wonderful. Ferris quotes John Archibald Wheeler: "To my mind there must be, at the bottom of it all, not an equation, but an utterly simple idea. And to me that idea, when we finally discover it, will be so compelling, so inevitable, that we will say to one another, 'Oh, how beautiful. How could it have been otherwise?'"[33]

The beginning of the universe has been approached scientifically by two related hypotheses, quantum genesis and vacuum genesis. The pioneer of quantum genesis is Stephen Hawking, who holds Newton's chair as Lucasian Professor of Mathematics at Cambridge University.

It was Hawking, together with British physicist Robert Penrose, who played a large part in the formulation of the essential features of the big bang theory of the origin of the universe. Between 1965 and 1970, they focused their attention, using the theory of general relativity, on black holes, the ultimate fate of massive stars that had exhausted their fuel. In such a star, the gravitational field at its surface becomes progressively intensified as contraction proceeds, and light rays are finally bent so strongly that they cannot escape. Since relativity specifies that nothing can exceed the speed of light, nothing can escape the gravitational field, and we have what must be a singularity of infinite density and space-time curvature. Hawking pointed out that this was "rather like the big bang at the beginning of time."[34]

However, Hawking has since changed his mind. In particular, he has proposed that what occurred in the first moments of the origin of the universe was not a singularity, a once-and-for-all, unique event, but instead a quantum fluctuation.[35] The impetus for this reexamination comes in part from the frustration that cosmologists feel in seeking to understand physical processes as a singularity. Ordinary physics just does not work at the extremes of energy and density and subatomic dimensions that occur. At this point, the force of gravity, which can be ignored in considering many physical processes, becomes the major factor. In most of the discussion of unification of the forces, gravity was ignored because it is ordinarily such a weak force in the context of particle-field interactions. However, at the high densities at the start of the big bang, gravity was the major force, just as it is at the collapse of a star to form a black hole. Not only was the force of gravity an important component of the first moments of the big bang, but the quantum dimension was considered a crucial factor as well. The problem with bringing in quantum theory is that gravity and quantum behavior are described by Einstein's general theory of relativity and quantum mechanics respectively, two theories inconsistent with each other. For this reason Hawking proposes a new quantum theory of gravity. This theory makes it possible that the ordinary laws of physics hold everywhere, including the beginning of time. There may be no necessity to postulate new laws for singularities, because, as Hawking explains it, there need be no singularities in the quantum approach.[36]

Hawking's proposal was first proposed in a lecture he gave in Padua, where Galileo used to lecture, in 1983. Timothy Ferris describes it as follows:

> What emerged was a tale of cosmic evolution possessed of a strangely alien beauty. All world lines diverge from the singularity of genesis, Hawking noted, like longitude lines proceeding from the north pole on a globe of the earth. As we travel along our world line we see the other lines moving away from us, as would an explorer sailing south along a given longitude: this is the expansion of the universe. Billions of years hence the expansion will halt and the universe will collapse, eventually to meld into another fireball at the end of time. There is however, no meaning to the question of when time began, or when it will end.[37]

In commenting on the globe analogy at another time, Hawking said that if the suggestion that space-time is finite but unbounded is correct, then the big bang is like the North Pole of the earth. If we ask what happens before the big bang, it is as meaningless as asking what happens on the surface of the earth one mile north of the North Pole.[38]

Hawking points out that there is not yet a complete and consistent theory that combines quantum mechanics and gravity.[39] However, one of its features would include physicist Richard Feynman's "sum of histories" approach to quantum mechanics. A particle does not have just a single history in quantum mechanics, as it does in classical theory. Instead, it is supposed to follow every possible path of space-time. So by calculating all possible trajectories of a particle, we arrive at the most probable description of how it reached its present observed state. However, when these calculations are made, serious technical difficulties arise. Their solution is to sum up only those histories that take place in what is called imaginary time. Actually, Hawking assures us that imaginary time is a well-defined mathematical concept. There are special numbers that give negative numbers when multiplied by themselves (one is called i, and when multiplied by itself gives -1, $2i$ multiplied by itself -4, and so on). For the sum of histories one must, for the purposes of calculation, measure time using imaginary numbers instead of real ones. The curious result is that the distinction between time and space disappears.

A second feature of Hawking's quantum theory of gravity is the use of Einstein's idea of the gravitational field as represented by curved space-time. When Feynman's sum of histories is applied, the analog of the history of a particle is now a complete curved space-time that represents the history of the universe.

Hawking tells us that the end result of combining these features—a sum of histories in imaginary time, and curved space-time—is to add one more possibility to the ways the universe can behave. In addition to an infinite existence or to its beginning in a singularity at some time in the past, it is possible in a quantum theory of gravity, with the time directions on the same footing as directions in space, for space-time to be finite in extent and yet have no singularities that formed a boundary. Going back to the global analogy, Hawking says "even though the universe would have zero size at the North and South Poles, these points would not be singularities any more than the North and South Poles of the earth are singular. The laws of science will hold at them, just as they do at the North and South Poles on the earth." [40]

The question of distinction between real and imaginary time remains. In what sense is the "mathematical device" of imaginary time valid?[41] Hawking suggests that it may even be more basic than real time:

> This might suggest that the so-called imaginary time is really the real time, and that what we call real time is just a figment of our imaginations. In real time, the universe has a beginning and an end at singularities that form a boundary to space-time and at which the laws of science break down. But in imaginary time, there are no singularities or boundaries. So maybe what we call imaginary time is really more basic, and what we call real is just an idea that we invent to help us describe what we think the universe is like.... But a scientific theory is just a mathematical model we make to describe our observations: it exists only in our minds. So it is meaningless to ask: Which is real, "real" or "imaginary" time? It is simply a matter of which is the more useful description.[42]

Ferris gives us some additional perspective on the significance of imaginary time:

> Imaginary time in Hawking's view was the once and future time, and time as we know it but the broken-symmetry shadow of that original time. When a hand calculator cries "error" upon being asked the value of the square root of -1, it is telling us, in its way, that it belongs to *this* universe, and knows not how to inquire into the universe as it was prior to the moment of genesis. And that is the state of all science, until we have the tools in hand to explore the very different regime that pertained when time began.[43]

Perhaps Hawking's most persistent concern is to analyze the role for a Creator in the universe that physics seems poised to define. In particular, he says that he, as Einstein before him, wants to know the mind of God. At one point he suggests that the success of scientific descriptions has led most people to believe that God allows the universe to evolve according to a set of laws and does not intervene to break those laws. This leaves the Creator with only the beginning of the universe as a province for activity. And yet at the point of a discussion of a no-boundary universe, he seems to see no role for God at all.[44]

At the conclusion to *A Brief History of Time*, Hawking continues this line of reasoning, recalling that Einstein had once asked if God had had any choice in constructing the universe, and concluding that if the no-boundary proposal is correct, the answer would be no. Admittedly, God would still have had the freedom to choose the laws of the universe, though even here it is suggested that God would be constrained by the paucity of theories that hold any promise to explain all the complicated structures of the universe, including ourselves.

This seems an odd way to talk about God, as though his creativity depended on our ingenuity. But Hawking does go on to the larger questions of why we and the rest of the universe exist. The answer he says, will be science's and human reason's ultimate triumph, for we shall know the mind of God.

From our perspective, the complementary view of origins that theology provides lends depth and breadth to any consideration of the mind of God. This universe is here for a purpose; it bears a grand design. And if we really wish to know God's thoughts, we must be prepared to be humbled by our own ignorance of the awesome immensity of what he has spoken into being.

Here, just as with our consideration of particles and fields in the previous chapter, we are confronted by a universe that surprises us with its intricacy and its elusiveness. For James Maxwell, his brilliant conception of electromagnetism as a field of force was not a cause to set God aside, but rather his faith in God was the very basis for examining novel explanations for his data, to see if they measured up to the richness to be expected from the Creator's mind.

Likewise, Julian Schwinger cautions us to maintain a deep sense of humility in the present rush toward a unified field theory. The presumption of full knowledge, to assume that we have an adequate understanding of how nature works—what all the energies are—denies the entire history of physics.

Timothy Ferris provides a cosmological perspective:

> We might eventually obtain some sort of bedrock understanding of cosmic structure, but we will never understand the universe in detail; it is just too big and varied for that. If we possessed an atlas of our galaxy that devoted but a single page to each star system in the Milky Way (so that the sun and all its planets were crammed on one page), that atlas would run to more than ten million volumes of ten thousand pages each. It would take a library the size of Harvard's to house the atlas, and merely to flip through it, at the rate of a page per second, would require over ten thousand years.

Add the details of planetary cartography, potential extraterrestrial biology, the subtleties of the scientific principles involved, and the historical dimensions of change, and it becomes clear that we are never going to learn more than a tiny fraction of the story of our galaxy alone—and there are a hundred billion more galaxies. As the physician Lewis Thomas writes, "The greatest of all the accomplishments of twentieth-century science has been the discovery of human ignorance."[45]

Perhaps some day we will have, as Stephen Hawking dearly hopes, a complete theory of the universe. But before it will gain the wider acceptance of the physics community, that theory will have to be backed by experimental data. Thus far, as Georgi and Schwinger and Dyson and Wheeler have all agreed, there is very little of the latter! And, as we have said, that data, as all of our scientific data, will lack the level of precision we once expected of it.

In the final analysis, we think it likely that even the most sophisticated and well-substantiated unified field theory will not give us more than a tiny inkling of the mind of God. For it will be *our* theory, and so of necessity only a human idea that refers to and seeks to express a profoundly deeper Reality.

Summary

Our goal in this chapter in examining the drive toward a unified theory of the forces of nature has been to demonstrate that a clear picture of physical reality eludes us here as well. Symmetry and symmetry-breaking have become valuable concepts for understanding physical forces, and the idea of a unity of the four forces—electromagnetism, the strong and weak nuclear forces, and gravitation—in a perfect symmetry at the beginning of the universe is a fascinating extrapolation. Thus far the only experimental verification comes from the demonstration of force particles associated with a combination of the electromagnetic and weak nuclear forces—the electroweak force—but the energies required for demonstrating earlier symmetries in the history of the origin of the universe are prohibitive. Thus a serious decoupling of theory from experiment exists, and again a scientific description of physical reality escapes us.

4

Self-Organization in the Evolution of the Cosmos

I. A Creative Universe

If the unity of nature is indeed one of the indispensable presuppositions of mankind, then we can appreciate the search for principles that link all the forces of nature in a grand beginning. But there is much more to our universe than its grand beginning in a big bang, however that is theorized to have come about. For what follows the beginning is a most astounding story of creativity throughout time, from the void of space to galaxies, planets, crystals, life, and people. The agency of this transformation has been called self-organization, and its exquisite products strongly suggest that something quite beyond random forces is involved. Paul Davies tells us in *The Cosmic Blueprint*[1] that for three centuries science has been ruled by the Newtonian and thermodynamic paradigms, which describe the universe as either an unchanging and sterile machine, or as a process moving inexorably toward degeneration and decay. Now we are presented with a new paradigm, a creative universe, whose processes are collective, cooperative, and organizational.

II. Unity and Diversity

Various authors have proposed explanations for the slow realization on the part of scientists and philosophers of the general significance of the creative paradigm. Physicist Freeman Dyson, in his book *Infinite in All Direc-*

tions,[2] has suggested that the search for simple solutions, a time-honored approach in science, has led scientific exploration toward what appeared to be the clear air of the mountaintops. Indeed, the great discoveries like Maxwell's equations for the electromagnetic field and Einstein's theory of general relativity towered above the landscape, and science seemed close to complete explanations. But, as Dyson says, "God did not only create mountains, he also created jungles…and we are beginning to understand that the jungles are the richest and most vibrant part of his creation."[3] It has been only in the past forty years that science has begun to explore seriously the valleys—the jungles—with their tangle of strange exceptions to our attempted generalities. So today, instead of three species of elementary particles, by Dyson's reckoning we have sixty-one. Instead of three states of matter, solid, liquid, and gas, we now have six or more. Now it is suggested that subatomic particles are represented by one-dimensional curves called "strings," and that burned-out stars will undergo gravitational collapse, perhaps existing forever as mysterious structures called "black holes." Dyson tells us that physicist Stephen Hawking has now succeeded in providing a coherent picture of black holes from both a gravitational and a thermodynamic point of view, so that black holes are no longer a mathematical abstraction, but his new theory is far from being mathematically precise and even further from being experimentally verified. Dyson says, "It leaves the mystery of black holes deeper than ever."[4]

Indeed, the gradual growth of complexity has been apparent throughout the history of science, but it was given a powerful framework for explanation in the middle of the last century through the evolutionary theory of Charles Darwin and Alfred Russel Wallace. These investigations focused their interest on the changes of living forms as a function of time, and we will devote future chapters to these biological aspects. But with the advent of cosmological science, it has become clear that the ideas of increased complexity and diversity inherent in biological evolution have also been characteristics of the entire universe of space and time. What appears to be the case is that the universe has never ceased to be creative, fashioning ever newer and more novel structures and relationships in the wondrous transitions from stardust to thinking humans.

Yet the world of physics has not accommodated readily to this point of view. The mountain climbers of the past like Einstein were unifiers, who believed that nature could be reduced to a finite set of equations. The diversifiers, who believed that nature is inexhaustible and infinitely complex, were few until recently. One of the pioneer diversifiers in physics was Emil Wiechert, who, speaking before the Economics Society of Königsberg in 1896, said:

So far as modern science is concerned, we have to abandon completely the idea that by going into the realm of the small we shall reach the ultimate foundations of the universe. I believe we can abandon this idea without any regret. The universe is infinite in all directions, not only above up in the large but also below us in the small. If we start from our human scale of existence and explore the content of the universe further and further, we finally arrive, both in the large and in the small, at misty distances where first our senses and then even our concepts fail us.[5]

Dyson also tells us that the dichotomy between the unifiers and diversifiers can be looked at in social terms, as the difference between the styles of academic science and industrial science.[6] He presents academic science as dominated by unifiers, and represents them by Athens, the first great academic city in the world. On the other hand, the science of the industrial world is represented by the first great British industrial city, Manchester, whose science was dominated by diversifiers. A particularly important historical point is that the growth of the diversity point of view in science in Manchester was not politically motivated by the Industrial Revolution, as has been suggested by some, but rather represented a scientific renaissance that was cultural and aesthetic. The perpetrators were medical doctors and Unitarian churchmen who formed an institution called the Manchester Library and Philosophical Society. The organization also attracted quality scientists of the day, including Joseph Priestley, John Dalton, and James Joule. It eventually gave birth to the University of Manchester and had a major share in the founding of the British Association for the Advancement of Science. Its members were generally antiestablishment, regarding with contempt the academic establishment of Oxford and Cambridge with its smattering of Latin and Greek, which marked a classical education. The science of the establishment—of Athens—emphasized ideas and theories, and sought unifying concepts to tie the universe together. The science that grew in the northern soil of Manchester emphasized facts and things, exploring and extending our knowledge of nature's diversity. The unification of science, had its great seventeenth-century spokesman in René Descartes and the diversifiers, on their part, were ably represented, in their first stirrings, by Francis Bacon. But the high noon for the diversifiers of Manchester came with the early 1900s when Ernest Rutherford was professor of physics at the University of Manchester. It was Rutherford who openly chided the Europeans for their insistence on abstract mathematics in deference to the use of physical models as a basis of description. But again he, as Weichert before him, were solitary voices for diversity.

In our last chapter, we described how the development of the universe from its earlier beginnings is regarded as a succession of symmetry-breakings. At its inception, the universe is symmetrical and featureless. As it cools, one symmetry after another is broken allowing more diversity of structure to develop. The formation of life, too, is a symmetry-breaking, changing the homogeneous mixtures of inanimate precursors into cells and organisms and eventually human beings and culture. For the mind of Athens, the interesting events are at the beginning, in the unity of the forces of nature. For the diversifiers, the view is forward, toward ever-increasing complexity and diversity of form. The farther we progress into the future, the more diversity of natural structures we will discover, and the more diversity of technology we shall create.

III. Explaining a Creative Universe

The great task that lies before us is the explanation for the enormous complexity and diversity of form in the cosmos. It would seem that the ability of the physical world to organize itself would involve fundamental and deeply mysterious properties. Philosopher Karl Popper says: "The greatest riddle of cosmology may well be…that the universe is, in a sense, creative." [7]

This creativity occurs not only in the vast reaches of space, but also at the levels of crystals and macromolecules and living cells, and, most of all, with people. The origins for such creativity, especially at the level of living things, seems hardly attributable to the sole working of the fundamental laws of physics. Recall that in chapter 1 we addressed the question of scientific explanation at different levels of complexity. There it was suggested that the various scientific disciplines may be distinguished by their position in a hierarchy of systems, with physics as the foundation followed by chemistry, biology, ecology, and so on. At each succeeding level the empirical content becomes enriched and new concepts appear that simply are not present at preceding levels. A strict reductionist would reject such a notion as the explanation for the gradual increase in complexity, but is hard pressed to explain biological phenomena like adaptation and natural selection in terms of the laws of physics, and utterly incapable of explaining such phenomena as consciousness and volitional behavior. However, it would seem that any scientific explanation involving higher-level laws must also be consistent with the lower-level laws that are of course simultaneously operating at that level. For example, an explanation of the function of the human brain in terms of a holistic pattern of electrical activity still must have charged particles and impulses behaving in a manner consistent with the fundamental laws of physics.

IV. The Concepts of Order and Time

But the idea that new concepts and laws appear with increasing complexity appears to have strong support. The whole really is greater than the sum of the parts. But can we extrapolate this holistic principle to postulate that there is a cosmic blueprint? Davies seems to think so, and to believe that it will one day be understood by the methods of science.[8] To approach this goal, we must look at what is presently known about the origin of order and organization in the universe.

The great edifice of physics that was built up in the seventeenth century, through the work of such pioneers as Galileo Galilei and Isaac Newton, is commonly referred to as classical mechanics. The great triumph of Newton was to demonstrate that his laws of motion correctly described the shapes and periods of the planetary orbits. In time it was assumed that if every particle of matter is subject to Newton's laws, with its motions determined by initial conditions and the forces acting upon it, then everything that happens in the universe is fixed in every detail. The universe is a clockwork! Everything that ever happened, is happening now, or will happen in the future has been unalterably determined from the first instant of time. The future is fixed! This was the sweeping implication of Newtonian mechanics!

In such a situation, what is the effect upon time? Davies tells us that if the future is determined by the present, then the future is in a way already contained in the present.[9] The present state of the universe contains the information for the future, and, by inversion of the argument, for the past too. All of existence is thus frozen in a single moment of time. Past and future have no real meaning. Nothing actually happens! Nothing *changes!* Such was the worldview of Newtonian physics. Yet we know from our own everyday experience that the world is changing, evolving. Past and future have real meaning. Things are happening. Time flows. Ilya Prigogine and Isabelle Stengers, in their book *Order out of Chaos*,[10] tell us that by the middle of the nineteenth century scientists were introducing new concepts that concerned heat engines and energy conversion in a new science called thermodynamics. Two laws were elaborated, one describing the conservation of energy and a second law that introduced the idea of disorder or entropy. The second law explained the frequently observed inefficiency associated with energy conversion. Some of the energy had been converted to an unusable form representing the increased molecular disorder of the system. The implication of the second law was far-reaching; there was an irreversible direction to natural processes. Time had an arrow. By contrast with classical mechanics, where time is reversible and past and future are indistinguishable, in thermodynamics, time is irreversible and past and future are distinctly different. Thus we understand the irreversibility of all natural phenomena as a consequence of the second law. Cooked eggs cannot be uncooked, we cannot reverse our own aging, and rivers do not flow uphill.

But this conclusion seemed to carry with it a very dire prediction. The universe is doomed. It is running down, inexorably approaching the eventual loss of all useful energy. This decay was said to have cosmic proportions because the sun and the rest of the stars are burning up their reserves of nuclear fuel and will finally grow dim and cold. This gloomy prognosis is called the "heat death" of the universe.

V. A Second Arrow of Time

But as we have been considering in this chapter, there is another arrow of time that lies alongside the thermodynamic arrow but points in the opposite direction. Its origin is mysterious, but its existence is strongly substantiated by the plethora of complexity and diversity of form all around us. The universe is progressing to ever more developed and elaborate states of matter and energy. This arrow should surely be called the optimistic arrow, as opposed to the pessimistic arrow of the second law.

How can these two opposite tendencies in the universe, neither of which can be denied, be reconciled? The answer is being found in a poorly studied category of earth's processes that are generally defined as nonlinear, far-from-equilibrium, and irreversible. Such processes are complex and irregular and difficult to study. The usual approach of modeling by approximation to regular systems is generally unsatisfactory, and the attitude on the part of most scientists has been to ignore complex reaction systems as unusual cases. Arthur Fisher, in an article in *Mosaic*, quotes a graduate student at Los Alamos National Laboratory's Center for Nonlinear Studies as saying:

> Your textbook is full of linear problems, and you become adept at solving them. When you're confronted with a nonlinear problem, you're taught immediately to linearize it; you make an approximation, use a special case. But when you venture into the real world, you realize that many problems are non-linear in an essential way and cannot be linearized meaningfully. You would just lose the physics.[11]

Paul Davies tells us that in fact the *majority* of processes in nature are nonlinear and that we must seek new approaches for their study:

> There is a tendency to think of complexity in nature as a sort of annoying aberration which holds up the progress of science. Only very recently has an entirely new perspective emerged, according to which complexity and irregularity are seen as the norm and smooth curves the exception. In the traditional approach one regards complex systems as complicated collections of simple systems. That is, complex or irregular systems are in principle *analysable* into their simple constituents, and the behavior of the whole is believed to be reducible to the behavior of the constituent parts. The new approach treats complex or irregular systems as primary in their own right. They simply cannot be "chopped up" into lots of simple bits and still retain their distinctive qualities.

We might call this new approach synthetic or holistic, as opposed to analytic or reductionist, because it treats systems as wholes. Just as there are idealized simple systems (e.g. elementary particles) to use as building blocks in the reductionist approach, so one must also search for idealized complex or irregular systems to use in the holistic approach. Real systems can then be regarded as approximations to these idealized complex or irregular systems.

The new paradigm amounts to turning three hundred years of entrenched philosophy on its head. To use the words of physicist Predrag Cvitanovic: "Junk your old equations and look for guidance in clouds' repeating patterns." It is, in short, nothing less than a brand new start in the description of nature.[12]

VI. New Order from Complex Structures

The salient thing about these complex processes is that they can give rise to new structures and new order spontaneously. For example, the flow of water from a faucet goes through a series of ordered structures as the flow rate is changed. Superconductivity in metals at certain low temperatures reveals a collective ordering of electrons. And living systems reveal a high level of order in far-from-equilibrium conditions. Many of the complex reactions fit into the category of chaotic behavior, and it is fascinating to realize that order and chaos can be so closely related. One of the most fascinating visual effects is seen in a chemical phenomenon called the "Belousov-Zhabotinsky reaction." When malonic acid, bromate, and cerium ions are placed in sulfuric acid in a shallow dish at certain critical temperatures, a series of pulsating concentric and spiral circles develop almost as if they were life forms. This behavior is the result of giant oscillations of millions of molecules, operating in concert, in the reaction system. The key feature of this kind of chemical phenomenon is the presence of autocatalysis: one or more of the reacting species is able to catalyze its own synthesis, and the whole system seems to pivot on this autocatalytic step. In contrast to chemical reactions in which reagents and products are distributed randomly in the solution, in the Belousov-Zhabotinsky type of reaction there are local inhomogeneities; in one region, one component may predominate, while in another part of the reaction vessel its concentration may be exhausted. The cooperative effect of a vast number of such reactant molecules leads to the pulsating, highly ordered arrangements. Prigogine and Stengers propose that these structures are the inevitable consequences of far-from-equilibrium reactions. The term Prigogine uses for this phenomenon is *order through fluctuation*.[13]

A simpler type of far-from-equilibrium chemical system is the chemical clock, studied by Prigogine and his collaborators by means of a model that he refers to as "brusselator." The model is distinguished by another

kind of catalytic feature, "cross-catalysis," in which two components recip-
rocally affect each other's synthesis. The fluctuations in this model system
are found to be of a highly specific periodicity, reflected in a remarkable
change in composition, from all of one component to all of a second component, practically instantaneously. Here we have an example of oscillations in time. In the Belousov-Zhabotinsky reaction the oscillations are
both time- and space-dependent, with waves of the two predominant species of molecules passing periodically through the system.

Another instance of order through fluctuation is the Bernard instability, in which one heats a liquid layer from the bottom and thereby establishes
a temperature gradient from bottom to top. At low-temperature differences
heat is transferred by conduction, and the fluid as a whole remains at rest.
But at some critical temperature value, a convection current appears spontaneously, and a huge cooperative movement of the molecules of the liquid
occurs, which takes the form of a grid of hexagonal cells. Prigogine empha-
sizes that according to the laws of statistics the original microscopic convection current should have been doomed to regression. Instead the minute
fluctuation is amplified until it invades the entire system. As Prigogine expresses it, "Beyond the critical value of the imposed gradient, a new molecular order has been produced spontaneously. It corresponds to a giant
fluctuation stabilized through energy exchanges with the outside world."

Davies describes a number of mathematical relationships that involve
simple manipulations of numbers leading to infinitely complex results.
Among these is the phenomenon of period doubling that is also known as
deterministic chaos.[14] It was first described by physicist Mitchell Feigenbaum, who found that only a limited number of patterns lead to chaotic
behavior. That is to say, transitions to chaos are ordered. Period doubling is
a process by which the periodic behavior of a system falters and becomes
erratic as a particular parameter, for example, temperature, is changed. In
the usual periodic process there is a fixed time interval between repetitions.
As some parameter is changed, this interval does not change gradually or
randomly, but doubles at each change. And the process of successive doubling is found to recur continually, until at a certain value of the parameter
under change, in Feigenbaum's words, "it has doubled ad infinitum, so that
the behavior is no longer periodic." Chaos has set in, but by a precise route
of period doubling. The fascinating thing about each period doubling is
that it represents a point at which a new level of order may be introduced,
just as in the cases of turbulent flow and the Bernard instability mentioned
earlier. What we have found is that the existence of complex and intricate
structures does not require complicated fundamental principles. Simple
equations that can be handled by a pocket calculator can give rise to an

extraordinarily rich variety and complexity. And these relationships are true for such diverse phenomena as turbulence in water and in the atmosphere, fluctuations of insect populations, behavior of a pendulum, and a chemical clock. We have also observed that such complex, dynamic systems very often display chaotic behavior. Finally, the evolution of such systems is exceedingly sensitive to the initial conditions, so that their behavior is essentially unpredictable. This is not to imply that the behavior of chaotic systems is intrinsically indeterministic. If we could fix the initial conditions, the entire future behavior of the system could be predicted precisely. But in practice we cannot specify the system exactly, and for chaotic systems this inaccuracy leads to a *magnification* of the error. In linear systems, errors grow in proportion to time. In chaotic systems, the errors grow at an escalating rate, exponentially with time.[15] But this essentially random element in complex systems is just the sort of situation one would desire for a truly creative mechanism, especially since the occurrence of chaos frequently goes hand in hand with the spontaneous generation of new spatial forms and structures. So nature can be both deterministic in principle, and random. But for all practical purposes determinism is a myth. As Prigogine says:

> The basis of the vision of classical physics was the conviction that the future is determined by the present, and therefore a careful study of the present permits an unveiling of the future. At no time, however, was this more than a theoretical possibility. Yet in some sense this unlimited predictability was an essential element of the scientific picture of the physical world. We may perhaps even call it the founding myth of classical science. The situation is greatly changed today."[16]

Davies summarizes:

> The conclusion must be that even if the universe behaves like a machine in the strict mathematical sense, it can still happen that genuinely new and in principle unpredictable phenomena occur. If the universe were a linear Newtonian mechanical system, the future would, in a very real sense, be contained in the present, and nothing genuinely new could happen. But in reality our universe is not a linear Newtonian mechanical system; it is a chaotic system. If the laws of mechanics are the only organizing principles shaping matter and energy then its future is unknown and in principle unknowable. No finite intelligence, however powerful, could anticipate what new forms or systems may come to exist in the future. The universe is in some sense open; it cannot be known what new levels of variety or complexity may be in store.[17]

A. THE SELF-REGULATING UNIVERSE

If we examine the night sky, there is little that suggests order. Stars appear to be scattered at random. If we use a small telescope, we find that stars are actually clustered in groups, sometimes as many as a million in a single aggregation. More powerful telescopes show that the nearer region of space is organized in a vast spiral-shaped system called the Galaxy, otherwise known as the Milky Way. Paul Davies tell us that there are about one hundred billion stars in our Galaxy and that it measures one hundred thousand light years in diameter. There is a distinctive structure, with a crowded central nucleus surrounded by spiral-shaped arms that are made up of dust and gas and some slowly orbiting stars. All this, we are told, is embedded in a large, more or less spherical halo of material that is for the most part invisible and of unknown character.[18] The general principles that lead to these aggregations are understood in terms of gravitational attraction, though the original source of the points of attraction remain unknown. But these galactic aggregations are not the largest structures encountered in the universe. Most galaxies are joined in clusters and even clusters of clusters. Davies tells us there are also huge voids and strings and sheets of galaxies.

At large-length scales, the universe takes on the appearance of uniformity. The best probe of the universe at large scale is the background heat radiation generated in the big bang. Recall from chapter 3 that the smoothness of this background radiation coming from all directions suggests that the universe is surprisingly homogeneous on the large scale. This has been assumed by astronomers for some time, and is known as the cosmological principle.

At the smallest astronomical scale, in our own solar system, the formation of the planets and the order and stability of their arrangement is a fascinating mystery. Several of the outer planets have their own miniature "solar systems" with multiple moons and, in the case of Saturn, a spectacular set of rings. The rings of Saturn form a huge planar sheet hundreds of thousands of kilometers in diameter and are composed of countless small orbiting particles. The Voyager Two space probe revealed a very intricate and complex superposition of thousands of rings, perhaps one hundred thousand in all, which were interrupted in orderly fashion by gaps, kinks and twists, and many embedded moonlets. Theoretical calculations suggest that the rings should be unstable, yet they appear to have been there for a billion years! Here is a remarkable example of the tendency for complex systems to develop and to establish high degrees of stability. The explanation for such behavior must include some of the same ideas of self-organization we have seen in the nonlinear, far-from-equilibrium processes that occur on the molecular scale.

B. The Third Revolution

Davies[19] tells us that there is a widespread feeling among physicists that their subject is poised for a major revolution. Twice before this has happened, once in the development of classical mechanics, and again with the advent of relativity and quantum theory.

Two programs are forging ahead with astounding speed. One is the reductionist program of the unifiers, seeking a total explanation for the nature of particles and fields. This has been dubbed a "Theory of Everything." It seeks the ultimate principles that operate at the lowest and simplest level of physics. The second program is the holistic program of the diversifiers, where the emphasis is on organization and function as integrated wholes. The key ideas here are complexity and organization rather than simplicity. The main question to be answered by the diversifiers is whether the propensity for matter and energy to self-organize can be explained by the known laws of physics, or whether completely new fundamental principles are necessary. Davies identifies three different positions on the part of the scientific community in dealing with the explanation of complexity and self-organization.

The first is the increasingly difficult position of complete reductionism, which asserts that there are no emergent phenomena, that ultimately all physical processes will be explained on the basis of the behavior of elementary particles and their interactions. Davies asserts that such a position is not only outmoded but leads to the exclusion of the most interesting directions for scientific investigation. In his words,

> Complete reductionism is nothing more than a vague promise founded on the outdated and now discredited concept of determinism. By ignoring the significance of higher levels in nature complete reductionism simply dodges many of the questions about the world that are most interesting to us. For example, it denies that the arrow of time has any reality. Defining a problem away does not explain it.[20]

A second position adopted by some scientists and philosophers is to reject reductionism and to propose that the existence of complex forms and systems is not a consequence of any relationship to lower-level laws, but is instead a totally original phenomenon. Thus philosopher Henri Bergson, though accepting the idea of purpose in the universe, rejects any notion that a fully described program is dictating the sequence of events.[21] True novelty, he says, is only possible if we have a continuously creative universe in which wholly new things originate in a way completely independently of what went before. Karl Popper also believes that creative processes like evolution, especially the evolution of life, are not derivative of what has gone before but are instead really novel. In his book with Sir John Eccles, titled *The Self and Its Brain*,[22] Popper talks about the novelty of evolution:

> The view that there is no new thing under the sun is, in a way, involved in the original meaning of the word "evolution": to evolve means to unroll;

and evolution meant originally the unrolling of what is there already: what is there, *preformed*, is to be made manifest. (To develop, similarly, means to unfold what is there.) This original meaning may be said to be now superseded, at least since Darwin, though it still seems to play its role in the world-view of some materialists....

Today some of us have learned to use the term "evolution" differently. For we think that evolution—the evolution of the universe, and especially the evolution of life on earth—has produced new things: *real novelty*.... According to present physical theory, it seems that the expanding universe created itself many billion years ago with a big bang. The story of evolution suggests that the universe has never ceased to be creative, or "inventive."...

The usual materialist view is that all the possibilities which have realized themselves in the course of time and of evolution must have been, potentially, preformed, or pre-established, from the beginning. This is either a triviality, expressed in a dangerously misleading way, or a mistake. It is trivial that nothing can happen unless permitted by the laws of nature and by the preceding state; though it would be misleading to suggest that we can always know what is excluded in this way. But if it suggested that the future is and always was foreseeable, at least in principle, then this is a mistake, for all we know, and for all that we can learn from evolution. Evolution has produced much that was not foreseeable, at least not for human knowledge.

Davies argues that this concept of uncaused creativity leaves the systematic quality of organization unexplained: "If new levels of organization come into existence without reference to what has gone before, why is there such orderly progression in a universe that has gone from featureless origin to rich diversity... Why should a collection of things which have no causes cooperate to produce a time-asymmetric sequence?"[23]

And then Davies goes on to point out that the answer that Bergson and Popper give cannot be called scientific, since it is the purpose of science to provide "rational universal principles for the explanation of all natural regularities."[24]

C. THE LAWFUL UNFOLDING OF ORGANIZED COMPLEXITY

The third point of view on the source of nature's organizing potency is that we must expect to find some physical principles in addition to the lower-level laws to explain its origin. Davies argues in support of this view on the basis that the gradual unfolding of organized complexity in the universe is a fundamental property of nature. Certainly it is not a rare property, for reactions that tend to lead to spontaneous self-organization are the norm in nature. He argues against the bias of regarding organizing principles in nature as shamefully mystical or vitalistic—and therefore unscientific—as "an extraordinary prejudice." He points out also that there is no reason why the fundamental laws of nature can only refer to the lowest level of laws. "There is no logical reason why new laws may not come into operation at each emergent level in nature's hierarchy of organization and complexity." Then Davies gives an example of the kind of organizing principles he has in mind:

> It is not necessary to suppose that these higher level organizing principles carry out their marshalling of the system's constituents by deploying mysterious new forces specially for the purpose, which would indeed be tantamount to vitalism. Although it is entirely possible that physicists may discover the existence of new forces, one can still envisage that collective shepherding of particles takes place entirely through the operation of familiar inter-particle forces such as electromagnetism. In other words, the organizing principles I have in mind could be said to *harness* the existing interparticle forces, rather than supplement them, and in so doing alter the collective behavior in a holistic fashion. Such organizing principles need therefore in no way contradict the underlying laws of physics as they apply to the constituent components of the complex system."[25]

D. The Computer Analogy

The computer has often been used to illustrate the fact that a given event may have two complementary descriptions at different conceptual levels, one represented by the hardware and the other by the software. The computer software program coexists with the computer circuitry, its hardware. Similarly, there exist software laws in nature, which govern the organization, information, and complexity of systems. These laws are fundamental and not derivable from the hardware laws of traditional fundamental physics, though they are compatible with those hardware laws.

E. Theology and Self-Organization

It is a common misunderstanding among scientists that a scientific explanation obviates any other explanation. That impression seems especially appropriate when the phenomenon is attributed to the "self," as though the entity in this case, experiencing an increase in organization, had premeditated its transformation. Of course, in scientific terms, the use of "self" actually connotes the absence of a clear relationship to some well-defined causal factor. But even if there was one, as Davies feels there will one day be shown to be, the question still remains: does a solid scientific explanation say all there is to be said? Is there no other side to the coin?

In the previous chapters of this book we have argued that science has changed dramatically in the past three decades, so much so that a "solid scientific explanation" of anything is an uncertain quantity if not a will-o'-the-wisp. Proof is something we no longer talk about in science. We can only ask for consistency in the picture of nature that science paints as a valid criterion for scientific truth.

The analogy of the artist and his painting has also been used in theology to explain and emphasize God's creative activity. Biophysicist Donald MacKay has pointed out that the biblical view of God's relationship to the world is far more intimate and dynamic than the nineteenth-century expositors' image of the machine tender. The God of Scripture is more like a super artist who can portray a constantly changing panorama of unfolding events in much the way that a television screen does. In his *Science and Christian Faith Today*, MacKay writes:

> The Bible as a whole represents God in far too intimate and active a relationship to daily events to be represented in…mechanical terms. He does not come in only at the beginning of time to "wind up the works"; he continually "upholds all things by the word of His power" (Hebrews 1:3). "In Him (i.e. Christ) "all things hold together" (Colossians 1:17). Here is an idea radically different from that of tending or interfering with a machine. It is not only the physically inexplicable happenings (if any), but the whole going concern, that the Bible associates with the constant activity of God….The whole multi-patterned drama of our universe is declared to be continually "held in being" and governed by Him.[26]

MacKay goes on to suggest the activity of God to be more like that of an artist than a machine tender. He says,

> An imaginative artist brings into being a world of his own invention. He does it normally by laying down patches of paint on canvas, in a certain spatial order (or disorder!). The order which he gives the paint determines the form of the world he invents. Imagine now an artist able to bring his world into being, not by laying down paint on canvas, but by producing an extremely rapid succession of sparks of light on the screen of a television tube. (This is in fact the way in which a normal television picture is held into being.) The world he invents is now not static but dynamic, able to change and evolve at his will. Both its form and its laws of change (if any) depend on the way in which he orders the sparks of light in space and time. With one sequence he produces a calm landscape with quietly rolling clouds; with another, we are looking at a vigorous cricket match on a village green. The scene is steady and unchanging just for as long as he wills it so; but if he were to cease his activity, his invented world would not become chaotic; it would simply cease to be.

> The God in whom the Bible invites belief is no "Cosmic Mechanic." Rather is He the Cosmic Artist, the creative Upholder, without whose continual activity there would be not even chaos, but just nothing. What we call physical laws are expressions of the regularity that we find in the pattern of created events that we study as the physical world. Physically, they express the nature of the entities "held in being" in the pattern. Theologi-

cally, they express the stability of the great Artist's creative will. Explanations in terms of scientific laws and in terms of divine activity are thus not rival answers to the same question; yet they are not talking about different things. They are (or at any rate purport to be) complementary accounts of different aspects of the same happening, which in its full nature cannot be adequately described by either alone.[27]

The scientific explanation for self-organization in the universe in terms of higher-level laws that are consistent with more fundamental laws is thus not a rival answer to the question of creation, but is instead more of an expression—in this case a somewhat tentative one—of the ongoing immanent activity of the Cosmic Artist who continues to bring his world into being. This dynamic view of God's activity opens up the possibility for a whole new view of the Creator's character and purposes in the universe. Certainly, strict adherence to a rigid plan seems inconsistent with the curiously experimental and opportunistic nature of the self-organizing universe.

Summary

In chapters 2 and 3 we have encountered the subatomic world as a seething mass of virtual particles, a world perhaps best described as an intricate pattern of wave forms in constant interplay. Now, in our consideration of the physicochemical processes of nature at the molecular level we are again surprised by the appearance of a novel phenomenon, by what has been called self-organization. The chemical sciences of a few decades ago emphasized a world in spontaneous decay whose processes were assumed to be linear and perfectly predictable. Now all that has changed. What we find in nature instead is a preponderance of nonlinear processes capable of subtle spontaneous interchange between ordered and chaotic states. The thermodynamic arrow in the direction of decay is seen to be opposed by a powerful thrust of natural processes toward new and highly diverse forms of ordered structures. And the extreme sensitivity of these processes to the initial conditions makes predictability to all intents impossible.

Again reality in the form of objective data and unambiguous explanation eludes us. The world is a far stranger and more baffling place than we had thought—full of creative surprise—even to the point of generating sentient beings such as ourselves! It is not difficult to sense something far more imaginative, purposeful, and powerful going on.

Perhaps in the future it will be possible to describe these wondrous phenomena in far more sophisticated scientific terms. But we are inclined to think that a full scientific description will still elude us, because the true definition will require knowledge of the infinite God of the universe, whose reality we only dimly perceive while he "holds in being" the universe.

5

Self-Organization and the Origin of Life

I. Introduction

The preceding chapters have considered ways in which current science has revealed a physical world far stranger and more elusive than we could have ever expected just a few decades ago. The reality we had sought in terms of precision and predictability has not been realized. Instead, the world has become overwhelming in both its size and its intricacy.

When we come to the beginnings of biological life, to questions of origins of biological complexity and the role played by self-organization, we are again confronted by the unpredictable and the utterly surprising. We might wonder what strange combination of events could have brought together nonlinear and autocatalytic reactions of such potential diversity as to lead to the plethora of organisms we call life?

To begin to answer these questions, we need first of all to look at the living system, to examine its special qualities, to look for the fundamental requirements that might have been present somewhere in the primeval earth some 3.8 billion years ago.

II. Molecular Biologist's View of the Living System

A. A Simple Definition

The living cell that molecular biologists have described in the past few decades is a profoundly intricate replicating metabolic system that is very simply described as an entity capable of generating energy in the biologically useful form of adenosine triphosphate for the purposes of producing enzymes, membranes, and organelles to conduct its metabolic functions and to reproduce its entire structure. The machinery of metabolism is fundamentally protein in nature, but its origin is based on a protein-synthetic system that takes its instructions from the cell's genetic information, encoded in its DNA. So we will first examine the nature of genetic systems.

B. Molecular Genetics

The explosive increase in our knowledge of the cell's genetic machinery began in a very quiet little garden in an Austrian monastery in the city of Brunn in the year 1865. The experimenter was Gregor Mendel, a monk, and his ten years of work, presented at the Natural History Society of Brunn, was scarcely noticed. But what Mendel discovered was truly earthshaking—that characteristics in his pea plants such as seed color or shape, and pod color or shape, were inherited as separate entities and were expressed in either of two ways that he designated "dominant" and "recessive."

Dominance was observed in the first genetic cross. If, for example, plants with smooth seeds were crossed with plants having wrinkled seeds, then the first or "F_1" generation displayed only one of the two seed shapes, that of the smooth or "dominant" character. Crossing hybrid plants led to a surprising result, the reappearance of the "missing" or recessive characteristic—unchanged—in one-quarter of the progeny. Mendel's conclusion was that there existed a fundamental unit of heredity that was carried intact through the generations. Later those units would be called genes.

But an appreciation of Mendel's discoveries did not come about until 1903 when a visual basis for inheritance came about with the discovery of chromosomes as structures with properties that exactly corresponded with Mendel's units of inheritance. Chromosomes could be observed prior to cell division to be divided longitudinally into two copies, and each copy to be subsequently pulled toward opposite poles of the cell. In this way each daughter cell received one copy of each chromosome—a complete set of genetic instructions.

The nonprotein components of genetic material had been the subject of a study, carried out by Friedrich Miescher in Basel, in the same time period as Mendel. Miescher had studied the nuclear material from two very different sources, the sperm of the Rhine salmon and pus cells from bandages from the local hospital. Both contained a substance he called "nuclein," which many years later was shown to be DNA. He also described another component of the salmon sperm, a very basic protein called protamine.

Protamine had the usual structure of a protein molecule, a long series of amino acids linked to each other in so-called peptide linkage, but there was a preponderance of basic amino acids—arginine, lysine, and histidine.

These, then, were understood as the fundamental components of the chromosome—a variety of basic proteins called protamines and histones and some less well characterized organic phosphorus compounds.

The genetic aspect was generally assumed to reside in the protein components, but in 1944 O.T. Avery and his collaborators, at what was then the Rockefeller Institute, demonstrated that a strain of the pneumonia-causing bacterium, pneumococcus, could be transformed from a nonvirulent to a virulent type by a nonprotein component of chromosomelike material obtained from the virulent type. This substance was shown to be the highly polymerized phosphorus-containing compound deoxyribonucleic acid (DNA).

The unique character of DNA as the conveyer of hereditary information was finally and unequivocally established in 1953 with the publication of the Watson-Crick model for DNA (fig.1). The structure of DNA at once suggested its hereditary role—two helical chains in which nitrogenous bases attached to the sugar-phosphate backbone of each chain were bonded to each other by weak, so-called hydrogen bonds. The bases were of four kinds called adenine (A), guanine (G), cytosine (C), and thymine (T), and bonding was specific. Each time an A appeared in one chain, a T was found opposite it. Likewise, each time a G occurred in one chain, a C was on the other. This system of complementary base-pair formation—A always opposite T and G opposite C, immediately suggested the basis of a hereditary mechanism. If the chains of nucleotides—as bases attached to their sugar phosphates are called—were separated and a new copy of each fashioned according to the base-pairing rules, the original molecules would be exactly reproduced. Presumably, too, the sequences of bases in the polymer were the information content of the molecule. Studies of mutation in which a single base was changed showed that the exact linear sequence was essential for proper functioning of the gene. The story of how Watson and Crick arrived at the structure of DNA reads more like a spy thriller than a journal article. In one of the great ironies of scientific research, the principal contributors of the data—Rosalind Franklin, the crystallographer whose data revealed the double helix, and Erwin Chargaff, the organic chemist who discovered the equality of A and T and of G and C— were bypassed, essentially by their own choice. They simply did not take the biochemist James Watson and his physicist friend Francis Crick—a kind of scientific "odd couple"—seriously.[1]

But once DNA's role in heredity had been established, another question loomed large. If DNA is the genetic material, then its role must be to direct the synthesis of all the cell's proteins. Yet protein synthesis was known to occur in the cell's cytoplasm, while DNA was restricted to the cell nucleus. How then did DNA transmit its instructions?

The answer to this question was first formulated by François Jacob and Jacques Monod, two French biochemists working at the Pasteur Institute. They were studying a fascinating bacterial phenomenon called induction, in which a new degradative enzyme was produced by growing cells when a substance was introduced into the culture medium that could be broken down and utilized for growth under the agency of that degradative enzyme. Furthermore, the process was reversible. On removal of the substance serving as a food source, the degradative enzyme quickly disappeared from the bacterial cells. Perhaps the most interesting aspect was that the induction process was under genetic control. The gene that produced the degradative enzyme was regulated by a second, closely linked gene. The French biochemists hypothesized that the gene producing the degradative enzyme was copied to form an intermediate template that was unstable, being constantly broken down and resynthesized. This molecule was proposed to be made up of ribonucleic acid (RNA), a close relative of DNA, which had been found in high concentration at the site of protein synthesis in growing bacteria.

Subsequently it was shown in several laboratories that DNA was actually copied into a polymer called messenger RNA (mRNA), again by complementary base pairing to ensure a faithful copy, by an enzyme system called "RNA polymerase." Enzymes called "DNA polymerases" had previously been described that were responsible for copying DNA, and they used so-called deoxynucleoside triphosphates, activated forms of the A, T, G, and C bases attached to the sugar unique to DNA, 2-deoxyribose. The RNA polymerase used a similar set of precursor molecules, A, U (uracil), G, and C, but this time the sugar was ribose instead of deoxyribose. Verification that this mRNA molecule was the "transcript" of the genetic material was obtained by demonstrating its movement form the site of synthesis in the nucleus to the protein-synthetic machinery in the cytoplasm. This machinery consisted of a complex structure called a polysome, made up of a series of so-called ribosomes attached to the long mRNA molecule, rather like pearls on a necklace.

It had also been shown that there was a direct linear relationship between the DNA sequence of a given gene and the amino-acid sequence of the protein for which that gene coded. In 1961, Nirenburg and Matthai, found that synthetic RNA molecules could catalyze the protein synthetic

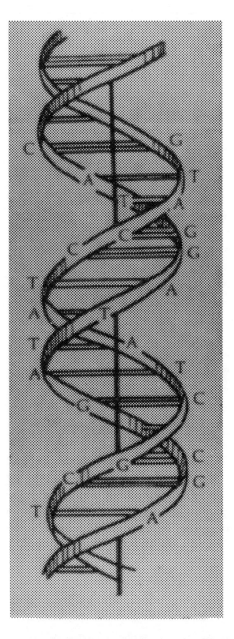

Figure 1.   A schematic representation of the double helix of DNA illustrating the complementary base pairing of adenine (A) with thymine (T) and guanine (G) with cytosine (C).

process in simple cell-free systems derived from bacteria.[2] The synthetic polynucleotides, produced with an enzyme called polynucleotide phosphorylase, could be made with various combinations of the component building blocks of natural RNA and then the protein synthesized subsequently from these compounds in the cell-free system could be analyzed. In this way it was discovered that the code signal for the insertion of a given amino acid into a protein structure was a sequence of three nucleotide units of the polynucleotide. For example, three uridine nucleotides (a trinucleotide) in a sequence of the RNA specifies the positioning of one molecule of the amino acid phenylalanine in the sequence of the protein.

Later a more precise method of determining the coding sequence (the "codon") corresponding to a given amino acid was discovered, based upon the known involvement of a second type of RNA, transfer RNA (t-RNA) in protein synthesis (see fig. 2). This molecule was shown to occur in many forms, at least one for each amino acid found in proteins and to function by adapting its amino acid to the codon through a complementary sequence of nucleotides in its own structure. It was found that even in the absence of protein synthesis, the specific t-RNA molecules bind to complexes of ribosomes and messenger RNA. Furthermore the messenger RNA could be replaced not only by the synthetic polynucleotides used in the earlier experiments, but also by simple trinucleotides of precise structure. In this method a given trinucleotide representing a single codon could be examined for its ability to cause binding of various t-RNA molecules with their attached amino acids to the ribosome structure. Those t-RNA molecules that bound must have been able to recognize that codon as the position for insertion of their particular amino acid. In this way it was possible to assign each codon to a specific amino acid. Figure 3 represents the genetic code as worked out for the bacterium *Escherichia coli.* Several interesting features are apparent with respect to evolution. The first is the phenomenon called degeneracy. Note that for most of the amino acids there is more than one codon, e.g., phenylalanine (Phe) is coded for by both UUU and UUC. Reading across the top of the table, first position, U: second position U; third position U or C. For the amino acid serine (Ser), there are four possible codons, with a different code letter for each in the third position. That is, the third position can vary and specificity still be retained. Because of this variation, it has been suggested that the original code was a doublet instead of a triplet code. Variation in the third position would also allow for the cell to undergo mutational change without that change being necessarily lethal. CT stands for codons that cause termination of a peptide chain (chain termination) and CI stands for chain initiation. For CI the amino acid methionine serves as the initiating amino acid and in this case the me-

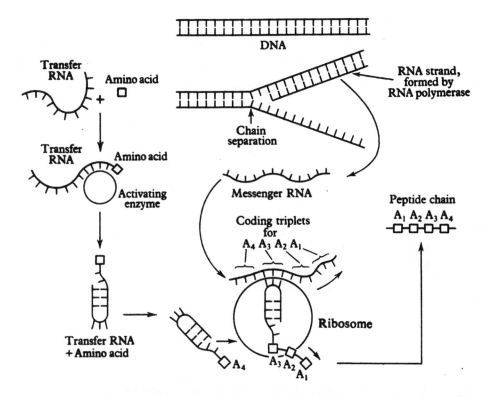

Figure 2.   The scheme for protein synthesis. DNA is "read out" in the
form of messenger RNA, which travels to the cytoplasm and
binds to structures called ribosomes. Here, a series of transfer
RNA molecules, at least one type for each protein amino acid,
carry their appropriate amio acid to the ribosome and align
with a specific coding sequence on the messenger to form the
proper sequence of the protein chain.

thionine is first formulated before initiating peptide synthesis. There are
also some interesting relationships between amino acids and their codons.
Similar amino acids (similar side chains) have similarities in their code words,
e.g., all nonpolar amino acids (phenylalanine, leucine, isoleucine, valine)
have U as the second code letter. Also, aspartic acid and glutamic acid,
closely related structurally, both have GA as their first two letters. This
suggested another evolutionary possibility: the specific code words for the
various amino acids arose because of some physicochemical relationship
between the codon's nucleotides and the amino acid that it specifies. This
possibility has been explored by a number of workers, but still remains to
be demonstrated.

	FIRST POSITION	SECOND POSITION				THIRD POSITION
		U	C	A	G	
Amino acid	U	Phe	Ser	Tyr	Cys	U
codons		Phe	Ser	Tyr	Cys	C
		Leu	Ser	(CT)	(CT)	A
		Leu	Ser	(CT)	Trp	G
	C	Leu	Pro	His	Arg	U
		Leu	Pro	His	Arg	C
		Leu	Pro	Gln	Arg	A
		Leu	Pro	Gln	Arg	G
	A	Ile	Thr	Asn	Ser	U
		Ile	Thr	Asn	Ser	C
		Ile	Thr	Lys	Arg	A
		Met (CI)	Thr	Lys	Arg	G
	G	Val	Ala	Asp	Gly	U
		Val	Ala	Asp	Gly	C
		Val	Ala	Glu	Gly	A
		Val (CI)	Ala	Glu	Gly	G

Figure 3. **The genetic code as worked out for the bacterium *E. coli.***

C. A UNIVERSAL CODE

Extension of these experiments to other bacteria, to intermediate forms, and to mammals, has led to the general conclusion that the genetic code is essentially universal—that the same code words are used in both lower and higher organisms. For example, with rabbit reticulocytes, twenty-two codons have thus far been shown to be translated into amino acids identical to those in the *Escherichia coli* bacterial system. The data though incomplete, point to a universal code.[3]

Likewise, the protein-synthetic mechanisms in prokaryotic and eukaryotic systems appear to be quite similar. For example, the chain-initiating codon that in the bacterium *Escherichia coli* involves a special form of transfer RNA, which places the amino acid methionine in the chain at that point, is also utilized by yeast, by wheat germ,, by mouse liver and rabbit reticulocytes. Other features of the mechanism also appear similar. The existence of a universal code could imply that there was indeed a single precursor of all living things, a primitive system capable of replication and information transfer from which all the present living forms developed.

D. CELLULAR METABOLISM

The simplest bacterium contains roughly three thousand different proteins, a thousand different RNA species (mostly messenger RNA) and perhaps another thousand different kinds of smaller molecules—including sugars and lipids and amino acids. The protein components may also be combined in various ways with sugars and lipids to form the structures of cellular membranes that enclose the cell and delineate its various compartments. Finally there are numerous cell organelles such as the ribosomes of protein synthesis and, in higher organisms, the mitochondria that serve as very efficient sources of energy for the cell. Figure 4 provides a simplified version of the structure of the much more complicated eukaryotic cell.

III. The Origin of the Living System

A. A HISTORICAL PERSPECTIVE

Twenty years ago one of us (Robert L. Herrmann) wrote an article on biogenesis that gave the impression that we were well on the way to a complete description of the origin of life:

> Science has made great progress in the area of origins. In addition to the growing weight of evidence for biological evolution, the biochemist has now described a chemical evolutionary counterpart of the biological model which likewise has enormous predictive and experimental value. All of the basic building blocks for biogenesis—the origin of life from inanimate matter—have already been shown experimentally to arise under primitive earth conditions. Amino acids, the components of proteins, and nucleotides, the components of nucleic acids, have been produced by simple reactions involving equally simple starting materials—those which were most likely present in the primitive environment of our planet. And more important, the formation of the complex macromolecules of living things—proteins, nucleic acids, polysaccharides and so on—may now be understood in terms of a continuous progression of increase in complexity, a chemical evolution, beginning with these basic structures. It is now most probable that the prebiological counterparts of the living system needed only an adequate energy source, one which we have every reason to believe was abundantly present (i.e., the sun); and that energy would prescribe a direction toward synthesis. For this is the unique quality of the living system—its unidirectional thrust toward organization, at the expense of the overall energy of the environment. The complex macromolecules, once formed, are surprisingly stable, especially so in the prebiotic situation. Given the added likelihood that some of the intermediate structures would have catalytic—even autocatalytic—activities, the explanation of the origin of a primitive living system by evolutionary mechanisms is well within sight. For such an evolving system, the long period of prebiological time is just what the doctor ordered; lots of time to experiment and innovate, with perhaps the first system to hit upon a nucleic acid—protein relationship as the winner among many participants.

> In other words, the living system need not have arisen full-blown; there are logical sequences of events which would have allowed for trial and

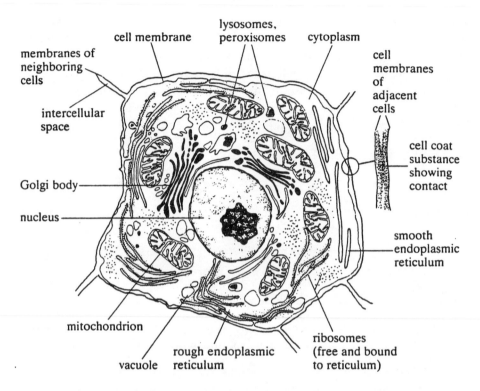

Figure 4. Simplified sketch of a generalized eukaryotic cell. Source: R.C. Bohinski, *Modern Concepts in Biochemistry*, 5th edition (Boston: Allyn & Bacon, 1987).

error within a given prebiological system, perhaps beginning with the synthesis of chains of nucleotide units—called polynucleotides—which has already been demonstrated under primitive earth conditions, and proceeding through amino acid activation, coupling to homologous fragments of the same polynucleotide system and protein synthesis.[4]

B. The Proposals for the Origin of Living Systems

The question of the origin of the living system has been addressed by a number of information theorists and biochemists examining possible primitive ribonucleic acid and protein structures. Paul Davies tells us, in *The Cosmic Blueprint*,[5] that the researchers have divided into two camps, those who favor the development of a genetic system first, and those who feel that proteins arose first and that genetic capability followed only gradually. Among the nucleic-acid-first group are Leslie Orgel of the Salk Institute and Manfred Eigen of the Max Planck Institute. Orgel has shown that nucleotides will under special conditions make RNA if they are given RNA molecules to copy, without any protein but with zinc ions as a catalyst. Eigen was able to accomplish the reverse process, demonstrating that RNA polymerases can under certain conditions make RNA from a mixture of precursor nucleotides without added RNA as a template. Thus far neither researcher has made RNA without having one or the other component—polymerizing enzyme or RNA—in the reaction mixture.

A proponent of the proteins-first school is Sidney Fox of the University of Miami. He has demonstrated the thermal formation of protein structures called "proteinoids" from mixtures of amino acids. These spherical structures display startling properties, the most striking of which is the capacity to bud and divide like living yeast cells.

Another of the proponents of the nucleic-acid first group is the information theorist Henry Quastler, who proposed in his *Emergence of Biological Organizations*[6] an ingenious mechanism for the origin of genetic information. In Quastler's proposal for the origin of the nucleic-acid system (fig. 5), nucleotide building blocks react with each other to form single polynucleotide chains. This process would be very slow in the absence of enzymes, but Quastler estimated that there would still be four hundred periods during geological time available for this reaction. The single chains thus formed may then react further with additional nucleotide units, by the nucleotide-pairing principle, to form intermediate structures that are partly single-chained and partly double-chained. This reaction is much more favorable than is the original reaction to form the single polynucleotide chain. Completion of this reaction leads to fully double-chained structures that may then reversibly separate to form single chains. The unique feature of such a system is that it gives rise to a kind of "information," in the sense that the first polynucleotide chain to be formed has a far greater chance for survival than any later arrivals. Thus it is able to compete more favorably for nucleotide units, since the reaction of the polynucleotide chain with nucleotides is favored over the original synthesis of the polynucleotide. The first chain thus becomes the progenitor of a unique polynucleotide system made up of itself and its "sister" chain, in which each nucleotide unit is the opposite pairing partner for the other chain—i.e., A opposite T and G opposite C. The information content of the system as Quastler saw it was of the nature of an "accidental thought remembered." The original arrangement of nucleotide units in the polynucleotide chain might have been arrived at by purely random interaction, but once the chain was formed, that particular arrangement and that of its sister strand were the only allowable structures. A good analogy would be the numbers of a combination lock.

ORIGIN OF A PRIMITIVE NUCLEIC-ACID SYSTEM

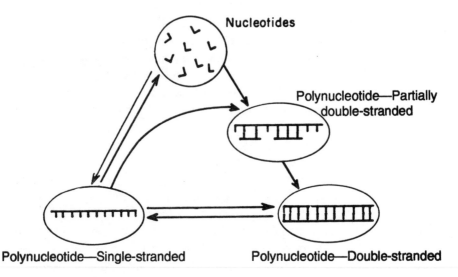

Adapted from : Quastler, "Emergence of Biological Organization"

Figure 5. Quastler's model for the origin of a nucleic-acid system. Nucleotides react to form single-stranded polynucleotides. The latter can undergo a more favorable reaction to form partially double-stranded structures that eventually give rise to a double-helical polynucleotide with a complementary base-paired structure. Adapted from: Quastler, "Emergence of Biological Organization."

Prior to their choice for the combination, the numbers are of no consequence. But after being introduced as the numbers of the combination they are now information.

The importance of Quastler's argument lay in its demonstration of the way in which the evolutionary principles of selection and competition can be applied at the chemical level. For here, from apparently random events, a system may be seen to arise that is capable of reproducing and propagating itself and hence acting as a kind of primitive genetic information.

The extrapolation of this scheme to an explanation for present mechanisms of protein synthesis may be made on the same principles of chemical evolution (fig. 6). Polynucleotides could react with amino acids with some degree of specificity,[8,9] to give adapter molecules similar to the amino acyl t-RNA's present in protein synthesis. Complementary base pairing of these

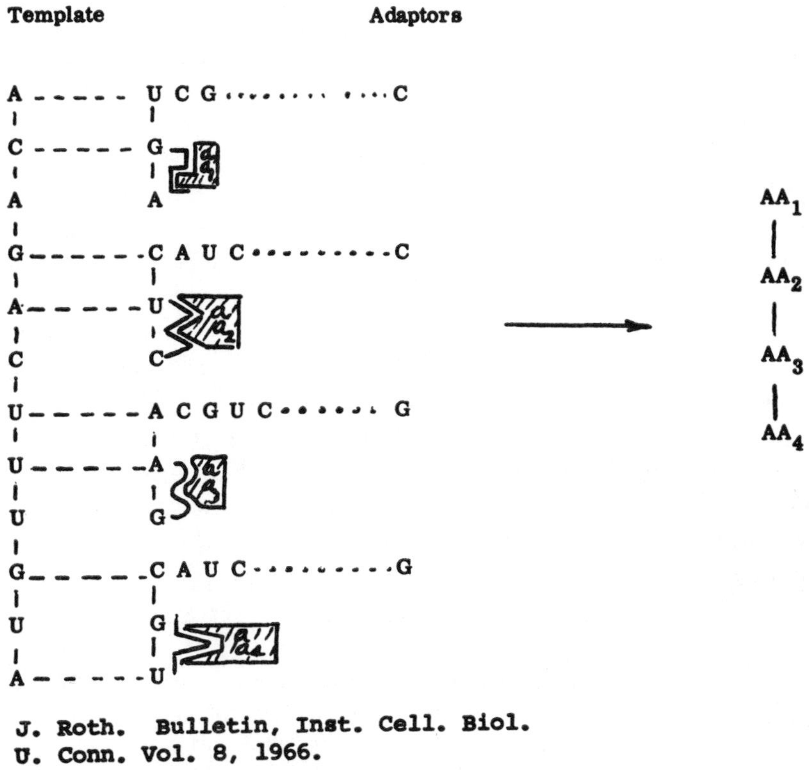

Template   **Adaptors**

Figure 6. A proposal for the attachment of primitive counterparts of amino-acid transfer RNA molecules to the template of a polynucleotide system, with the eventuality of the synthesis of amino-acid polymers. J. Roth.[7]

molecules to the original polynucleotide system would provide the opportunity for the system to couple amino acids in a variety of different arrangements, depending upon the sequence of the original polynucleotide, and if one or more amino-acid sequences proved to have enzymatic activity, there would be the tremendous advantage, by virtue of the self-duplicating property of polynucleotides, for this system to "remember" it.

Thus even the informational content of a living system may have arisen, in its simplest form, from the apparently random way in which the nucleotide building blocks of the first successful system were incorporated into a polynucleotide polymer. Considering the available data on the universality of the code and a theoretical framework for its origin, the description of life's origins in a purely mechanistic sense appeared to lie within the grasp of modern molecular biology.

C. A Changing Mood

The ensuing decades have not been kind to our earlier expectations. In fact, Robert Shapiro, in his 1986 book entitled *Origins—A Skeptic's Guide to the Creation of Life on Earth*, tells of the gloomy mood of the Seventh International Conference on the Origin of Life, held in Mainz, Germany, in 1983.[10] In fact, Shapiro's own paper was entitled "The Improbability of Prebiotic Nucleic Acid Synthesis." Many others expressed skepticism and there was general fear that funding, especially by the National Aeronautics and Space Administration, was ending. In fact, the extent of the impasse reached by research on biochemical origins is far greater, as revealed in a book entitled *The Mystery of Life's Origin: Reassessing Current Theories* by Charles Thaxton, Walter Bradley, and Roger Olsen.[11] The preface to this book is written by Dean Kenyon, author of an earlier, optimistic book called *Biochemical Predestination* concerning biochemical explanations for the origin of life.[12] Kenyon sees a disturbing trend in oversimplification in more recent studies, and confesses a deep concern about the theory of chemical evolution. He writes:

> The modern experimental study of the origin of the first life on earth is now entering its fourth decade, if we date the inception of this field of research to Stanley Miller's pioneering work in the early 1950's. Since Miller's identification of several (racemic) protein-forming amino acids in his electric discharge apparatus, numerous follow-up studies have been conducted. Conforming in varying degrees to the requirements of the so-called "simulation paradigm," these experiments have yielded detectable amounts of most of the major kinds of biochemical substances as well as a variety of organic microscopic structures suggested to be similar to the historical precursors of the first living cells.
>
> The experimental results to date have apparently convinced many scientists that a naturalistic explanation for the origin of life will be found, but there are significant reasons for doubt. In the years since the publication of *Biochemical Predestination* I have been increasingly struck by a peculiar feature of many of the published experiments in the field. I am not referring to those studies conducted more or less along the lines of Miller's original work, although there are firm grounds for criticizing those studies as well. I am referring to those experiments designed to elucidate possible pathways of prebiotic synthesis of certain organic substances of biologic interest, such as purines and pyrimidines, or polypeptides.
>
> In most cases the experimental conditions in such studies have been so artificially simplified as to have virtually no bearing on any actual processes that might have taken place on the primitive earth. For example, if one wished to find a possible prebiotic mechanism of condensation of free

amino acids to polypeptides, it is not likely that sugars or aldehydes would be added to the reaction mixture. And yet, how likely is it that amino acids (or any other presumed precursor substance) occurred anywhere on the primitive earth free from contamination substances, either in solution or the solid state? The difficulty is that if sugars or aldehydes were also present polypeptides would not form. Instead an *interfering cross-reaction* would occur between amino acids and sugars to give complex, insoluble polymeric material of very dubious relevance to chemical evolution. This problem of *potentially interfering cross-reactions* has been largely neglected in much of the published work on the chemical origins of life. The possible implications of such an omission merit careful study.

Other aspects of origin-of-life research have contributed to my growing uneasiness about the theory of chemical evolution. One of these is the enormous gap between the most complex "protocell" model systems produced in the laboratory and the simplest living cells. Anyone familiar with the ultrastructural and biochemical complexity of the genus *Mycoplasma*, for example, should have serious doubts about the relevance of any of the various laboratory "protocells" to the actual historical origin of cells. In my view, the possibility of closing this gap by laboratory simulation of chemical events likely to have occurred on the primitive earth is extremely remote.

Another intractable problem concerns the spontaneous origin of the optical isomer preferences found universally in living matter (e.g., L—rather than D—amino acids in proteins, D—rather than L—sugars in nucleic acids). After all the prodigious effort that has gone into attempts to solve this great question over the years, we are really no nearer to a solution today than we were thirty years ago.

Finally, in this brief summary of the reasons for my growing doubts that life on earth could have begun spontaneously by purely chemical and physical means, there is the problem of the origin of genetic, i.e., *biologically relevant*, information in biopolymers. No experimental system yet devised has provided the slightest clue as to how biologically meaningful sequences of subunits might have originated in prebiotic polynucleotides or polypeptides. Evidence for some degree of spontaneous sequence ordering has been published, but there is no indication whatsoever that the non-randomness is biologically significant. Until such evidence is forthcoming one certainly cannot claim that the possibility of a naturalistic origin of life has been demonstrated.[13]

Thaxton et al. go on to give a detailed critique of origin-of-life research and conclude that chemical evolution is highly implausible. They also add an interesting statement in their conclusion: "A major conclusion to be drawn from this work is that the undirected flow of energy through a primordial atmosphere and ocean is at present a woefully inadequate explanation for the incredible complexity associated with even simple living systems, and is probably wrong."[14]

We would of course agree that the marvelous transformations that are seen in living systems and in the nonliving systems considered in the last chapter—seem inexplicable without the active participation of a Divine Mover. Certainly, the present impasse invites fresh ideas and variations on the present schemes of biogenesis.

D. THE DOUBLE-ORIGIN HYPOTHESIS

One of the more recent theorists in the field is physicist Freeman Dyson, who discusses the origin of life in his book *Infinite in All Directions*.[15] Dyson, as we considered in the last chapter, is an apostle of diversity. For that reason he likes complexity, and sees in nature's creative complexity the opportunity to take fresh approaches to explore the inexhaustible riches of the universe. Dyson expresses the physicist's dislike for "the ugliness of chemical terminology," and chooses to "take refuge in metaphor," in this case the computer, as a representation of the chemistry of living systems.[16] The hardware of the computer is its electronic circuitry, which carries out logical or mathematical operations. Its software is the floppy disc on which instructions and information are written. Software is fed into hardware to tell the hardware what to do. By analogy, Dyson says, in the living cell there are two major components, proteins and nucleic acids. Proteins are the hardware of the cell, providing structure and performing as catalysts in highly specific reaction sequences. Nucleic acids are software, organizing the work of the proteins. Though the metaphor is an imperfect one (since nucleic acids code for proteins, software would be generating hardware) it can still be extended a little further. As we described earlier, living cells have two general functions—metabolism and replication. In the computer metaphor, metabolism represents hardware and replication software. Metabolism is the concern of protein and requires constant activity. Replication is a software function, since nucleic acids, like floppy disks, provide stability and legibility.

Dyson explains that the computer metaphor for the living cell was first used by the mathematician John Von Neumann in 1948. A pioneer in the theory of self-reproducing automata, Von Neumann defined two essential components of automata that were later called "hardware" and "software." As we said before, hardware processes information, whereas software embodies information. Von Neumann saw both components as essential for a complete self-reproducing automaton, but, most importantly, hardware was seen to come logically before software. An automaton composed of hardware alone can exist and maintain its own metabolism. On the other hand, an automaton composed only of software must be an obligatory parasite. It functions only when other automata are available that have hardware to lend. In the biological world, the example of an automaton with essentially only software is the bacteriophage, a bacterial virus that requires a host bacterium to carry out functions for which the virus carries its own instructions. Dyson brings this idea of hardware as primary and software as secondary to the question of origins. Could it be that the protein components and some metabolic scheme were the first "living" system, possessing also perhaps some primitive reproducing capability like that shown by Fox's proteinoids?[17]

To support this idea, Dyson points out that there is evidence that most of the internal structures of living cells did not originate within those cells but probably arose by invasion of independent living creatures behaving rather like current infectious agents. This theory, first presented by Lynn Margolis in 1981,[18] sees the gradual evolution of hosts and their invading parasites to a relationship of mutual dependence. The stages of this evolution would perhaps include a role for the invading disease organism as a chronic parasite, a symbiotic partner, and finally an integral part of the metabolic machinery of the host. Support for the Margolis theory comes from the fact that cellular structures like mitochondria are more closely related to bacteria than to the eukaryotic cells in which they are found.

The Margolis theory explains that most of the big steps in evolution were caused by parasites. In light of the double-origin hypothesis, nucleic acids appeared only after the living protein system was functioning and behaved as an invading cellular parasite. The original living creatures were cells with a metabolic apparatus but no genetic apparatus.[19]

The first picture of a protein-based origin was actually given some fifty years ago by the Russian chemist Alexander Oparin.[20] He proposed the order of events: cells first, proteins second, genes third. His fundamental observation, as Dyson describes it,[21] was that when a suitably oily liquid is mixed with water, it sometimes happens that the two liquids form a stable mixture called a "coacervate," with the oily liquid dispersed into small droplets in the water phase. These droplets superficially resemble living cells, and it was proposed that there was a gradual change to more complicated populations within the droplets of coacervate with time. Given some physical structure to function as a framework for the cell, coacervate droplets of a variety of metabolic potentials might be formed and organized into self-sustaining metabolic cycles.

Thus far there is no strong evidence favoring the protein-based origin of either Fox's proteinoids or Oparin's coacervates. But by putting metabolism first, the protein model escapes the major difficulty of nucleic acid-based origins that suffer from accumulation of errors with the eventual prospect of "error catastrophe." Unless the nucleic acid-based system functions in an almost error-free manner, errors will accumulate with each generation and the system will deteriorate to extinction. The protein model also appears favored by the relative ease of prebiotic synthesis of proteinlike components and the difficulty of the formation of nucleic acid-like components.

Dyson has constructed a theoretical model of the origin of life, based upon the Oparin theory.[21] It is a simple mathematical model that allows calculation of the probability of a primeval molecular population jumping between two states that differ by the presence or absence of metabolic organization. This situation is analogous to the distinction between life and death in biological systems. The ordered state of the population of molecules is "alive," since under this condition most molecules are collaborating to maintain the catalytic cycles of metabolism. The disordered state, where most cycles are inoperative, is considered "dead." It is the rare possibility of a large statistical fluctuation from one state to the other that is most interesting, for if the "dead" cell makes the jump from a disordered to an ordered state, the "origin of life" has occurred.

The model has three main ingredients. First, the molecular population is treated by the elementary equations describing the behavior of a biological population. Second, the rates of metabolic reactions are expressed based upon thermodynamic parameters. Finally, the order-disorder transition is treated statistically. When the model is examined for various values of the population of molecules, it is found that a population of several thousand building blocks linked into a few hundred large molecules provides sufficient variety for catalytic cycles to be formed. Most importantly, a population in the range of ten thousand is large enough to display complexity comparable to living systems yet still small enough to allow the statistical jump from disorder to order to occur with reasonable probability. And finally, Dyson points out in the following passage the real success of the model is in its ability to tolerate error:

> The basic reason for the success of the model is its ability to tolerate high error rates. It overcomes the error catastrophe by abandoning exact replication. It neither needs nor achieves precise control of its molecular structures. It is this lack of precision which allows a population of ten thousand building blocks to jump into an ordered state without invoking a miracle. In a model of the origin of life which assumes exact replication from the beginning, with a low tolerance of errors, a jump of a population of N building blocks from disorder to order will occur spontaneously only with

N of the order of one hundred or less. In contrast, a non-replicating model can make the transition to order with a population a hundred times larger. The error rate in the ordered state of our model is typically between 20 and 30 percent. An error rate of 25 percent means that three out of four of the building blocks in each molecule are correctly placed. A catalyst with five building blocks in its active site has one chance out of four of being completely functional. Such a level of performance is tolerable for a non-replicating system, but would be totally unacceptable in a replicating system. The ability to function with a 25 percent error rate is the decisive factor which makes the ordered state in our model statistically accessible, with populations large enough to be biologically interesting.[22]

The Dyson model has not been tested, but he believes that it can be. The question he would ask is, "Does there exist a chemical realization of my model, for example a population of a few thousand amino acids forming an association of proteins which can catalyze each other's synthesis with 80 percent accuracy? Can such an association of molecules be confined in a droplet and supplied with energy and raw materials in such a way as to maintain itself in a stable homeostatic equilibrium?"

But what if his model proves to be wrong? To this question Dyson replies with a quote from his favorite poet, William Blake: "To be an Error and to be Cast out is a part of God's Design." [23]

Dyson's application of the model to other areas of science is a fascinating one. He notes that the same question met in studies of the origin of life is encountered in ecology, economics, and cultural history as well. The question is, why is life so complicated? His answer is that homeostatic mechanisms, which are intrinsic to life, are involved in each of these other disciplines, and to be effective, homeostatic mechanisms must be complex. In ecology, the typical stable community of a few acres of woodland comprises thousands of diverse species with highly specialized and interdependent functions. The same is true for economic systems and societies. As Dyson expresses it:

> The open-market economy and the culturally open society, notwithstanding all their failures and deficiencies, seem to possess a robustness which centrally planned economies and culturally closed societies lack. The homeostasis provided by unified five-year economic plans and by unified political control of culture does not lead to a greater stability of economies and cultures. On the contrary, the simple homeostatic mechanisms of central control have generally proved more brittle and less able to cope with historical shocks than the complex homeostatic mechanisms of the open market and the uncensored press.[24]

Dyson tells us that the comparison of his first living system with the system of ecology was for the purpose of drawing a "biological moral." He notes that Charles Darwin used the image of the "tangled bank" at the end of his *Origin of Species* to describe the nature of life. Darwin described life as "an image of grasses and flowers and bees and butterflies growing in tangled profusion without any discernible pattern, achieving homeostasis by means of a web of interdependences too complicated for us to unravel." [25] The tangled bank is Dyson's image for the first living cell. And an essential part of that image is error-tolerance. The first cells were error-tolerant tangles of nonreplicating molecules. Replication was an alien and parasitic intrusion that came much later, imposing rigid control on the hardware. But the error-tolerance was not lost; it was transferred to the software. It was then the replicating system's turn to make errors and be creative, and with far greater freedom than its predecessor.

The "biological moral" to be drawn from the comparison of ecology and the first primitive cell is that nature is complicated and that something intrinsic in the error-tolerance of nature is fundamental to living systems at every level.

E. Implications of Error-Tolerance for Living Systems

A fascinating analogy has been drawn between the evolution of genetic systems and of human societies by Richard Dawkins in his book *The Selfish Gene*.[26] The main theme of the book is the tyranny of the replication apparatus in imposing strict control over all of evolutionary history. Every species is the captive of its own genes, and is compelled to develop and to behave in a manner that will maximize the survival of the genes. This tyranny is three billion years old, but in the last hundred thousand years it has been overthrown, by one species, *Homo sapiens*, which has developed language and culture and is now evolving on the basis of its culture rather than its genes.

Dyson reacts to this view of evolution as far too simple. Indeed we are in a sense rebels by nature, but our rebellion is more complicated than a revolt against our genes.[27] The replicators did not exist in the beginning, and even after the advent of the genetic system as the cell's software, there was always the pull of homeostasis and of error-tolerance in the tangled web of molecular structures to maximize diversity of structure and function.

Then, too, the transfer of error-tolerance to the replication system implies that the genes were "at risk" by the very nature of the nucleic acids of which they were made—sensitive to mutagens and eventually to a plethora of rearrangement mechanisms like genetic recombination and gene transposition. The picture is one that hardly suggests tyrannical control. The overall picture that Dyson paints is of a living system far more loosely structured and far less rigidly controlled than the Darwinian view. This "new and looser picture of evolution" is supported by recent experimental discoveries in molecular biology that have led Edward Wilson to describe the cell's genetic situation as "a rainforest with many niches occupied by a whole range of elements, all parts of which are in a dynamic state of change."[28]

The second implication of error-tolerance in living systems bears upon our concept of the Creator and his activity in the world. The feeling is often expressed that a world where chance and random error are foundational cannot be ruled by a faithful and omnipotent Creator. How can the apparently blind forces of disorder be an expression of the Creator's purpose? This question is addressed in a fascinating book written by physicist-theologian John Polkinghorne entitled *Science and Creation*.[29] He points out that the expression of purpose is not inconsistent with random forces if there is the interplay of chance with necessity, the production of novelty through random forces operating within a structure of law that selects and retains useful innovations in the ongoing process of evolution. In fact, the occurrence of chance and law—chance and necessity—is consistent with the character of God as both loving and faithful. His faithfulness is expressed in the laws that govern the evolutionary mechanisms. His love gives freedom to his creation for trial and error and innovation around the foundation of law and consistency.

IV. The Reality of Origins

The three decades of research on biogenesis since the first International Conference on the Origin of Life held in Moscow in 1957 have provided some fascinating ideas but very little meaningful data on the beginnings of life. Admittedly, the subject is of utmost interest to us because it cannot be separated from our own existence. And we have to believe as scientists that some scientific explanation does exist. But just what level of detail should we expect for what must have been and extraordinarily rare event, a unique event for which the distinction between natural process and miracle evaporates?

In this framework it is interesting to look again at some theoretical possibilities that as yet have no specific application to the problem. Paul Davies reminds us, in *The Cosmic Blueprint*, that several researchers of reputation have theorized that life arrived on our planet from outer space.[30] This is the suggestion of Nobel laureate physicist—molecular biologist Francis Crick, and of cosmologists Fred Hoyle and Chandra Wickramasinghe. In this connection it is interesting to note that traces of amino acids and of all five of the organic bases in DNA have been found in a meteorite that fell on Murchison, Australia, in 1969.[31] But nothing resembling the macromolecules of significance for life have thus far been found.

But Davies goes on to emphasize a third possibility,[32] that life arose on earth at bifurcation points under far-from-equilibrium conditions in nonlinear reactions of the kind described by Prigogine and discussed in the last chapter. If such remarkable behavior as is seen in the Belousov-Zhabotinsky reaction and in the chemical clock involves only relatively simple interactions of a few components, then how much more innovative should be the reactions of the "tangled mass" of biomolecules in the first primitive cell? This question takes on even greater significance if the poorly understood laws that govern fluctuations in nonlinear systems in far-from-equilibrium conditions should include additional organizing principles in the hierarchy of these more complex systems.

In any case, the mystery of life's origin is still with us after thirty years of intense study, and we suspect that the solution to the mystery, if and when it comes, will still invoke wonder and awe in those of us who are not surprised that reality is deeper than we are.

Perhaps Loren Eiseley said it best in his *Immense Journey:*

> Men talk much of matter and energy, of struggle for existence that molds the shape of life. These things exist, it is true; but more delicate, elusive, quicker than fins in water, is that mysterious principle known as organization, which leaves all other mysteries concerned with life stale and insignificant by comparison. For that without organization life does not persist is obvious. Yet, this organization itself is not strictly the product of life, nor of selection. Like some dark and passing shadow within matter, it cups out the eyes' small windows or spaces the notes of a meadowlark's song in the interior of a mottled egg. That principle—I am beginning to suspect—was there before the living in the deeps of water....

> If "dead" matter has reared up this curious landscape of fiddling crickets, song sparrows, and wondering men, it must be plain even to the most devoted materialist that the matter of which he speaks contains amazing, if not dreadful powers, and may not impossibly be, as Hardy has suggested, "but one mask of many worn by the Great Face behind."[33]

Summary

In this chapter we have looked at the biochemistry of the living system as we understand it now and we have tried to visualize how anything even remotely related could have originated. Extensive research in origins has not been very fruitful, and theoretical models like Dyson's suggest that the kind of homeostatic mechanisms characteristic of the simplest living systems would have been of necessity highly complex. Davies and Wilson concur that creativity of the kind involved in living systems seems to demand a high level of complexity. Darwin anticipated this when he referred to the "tangled mass" from which life originated. Eiseley talks of that mysterious principle known as organization which was "there before the living in the deeps of water."

Here again, as with particle physics, cosmology, and the search for the "theory of everything," we are forced to a recognition of profound complexity and mystery as we probe for reality. The most intriguing ideas and explanations seem to point beyond our science and beyond our theological constructions to an infinitely powerful Intellect Who oversees a profoundly creative and experimental drama. Based on what we now know about our universe, it would seem that we must entertain the possibility that we are perhaps only current players in a small "side show." But if this is so, the "main event" must be truly magnificent, and a reality we can scarcely imagine!

6

Self-Organization and
the Diversity of Life

I. Toward a Deeper Reality

We have now looked at the creative paradigm from the standpoint of the remarkable propensity of inanimate matter to self-organize and then to give rise to the first ancestor of the modern living cell. In all of this there is an overwhelming sense of mystery and wonder, as though reality is far deeper and more profound than we had thought. Indeed, the best of scientific investigation seems to be rewarded with wondrous insights of a greater universe of ever-increasing complexity and intricacy. The antitheist concludes that it is all a very remarkable happenstance, but that is all. The theist quite readily sees "the Great Face behind," but not without some question about the apparent false starts and blind alleys and even error-tolerance that seem essential parts of the evolutionary process.

When we turn to the subject of the evolution of life, the trail of surprises accelerates. Just thirty years ago biological evolution was assumed to follow the Darwinian view of gradual increase in complexity of organisms with time. Little was known of the earliest stages of evolution and a simple mechanism of natural selection among a series of chance mutations seemed reasonable. But just as with the research on the origin of life, the recent studies of the time course of appearance of organisms reveals a startling series of discontinuities. Life appears almost before the earth has had time to cool, and variety and complexity of form appear without the expected simpler precursor organisms.

II. The Evolutionary Paradigm

Louise Young, in her fascinating book, *The Unfinished Universe*,[1] describes the sequence of events in biological evolution as a remarkable interplay between an environment sometimes hostile, but more often incredibly supportive, and an amazingly adaptive and opportunistic series of life-forms. Indeed, the interaction between the actors in this drama is so creative that she describes it as "form set free to dance through time and space."[2]

The earliest data for living organisms is provided by fossils found in strata in Africa and in Western Australia dating back 3.5 million years. They appear to be the imprint of both simple bacteria and primitive unicellular photosynthetic organisms similar to the present blue-green algae. These organisms appear in "stromatolites," mats of sediment trapped in a network of algae and bacteria. The early advent of photosynthesis appears to have been critical. The atmosphere of the primitive earth apparently contained no free oxygen and no protective layer of ozone to screen out the damaging ultraviolet radiation from the sun. Prior to photosynthesis, simple living things survived in the depths, away from sunlight, utilizing crude mixtures of organic compounds formed by sunlight and lightning and volcanic action. Primitive membranes and enzymes enabled crude metabolic processes, but it is probable that life could not have survived with these components alone. Photosynthesis allowed living cells to use the sun's energy, together with atmospheric carbon dioxide, to carry out their metabolism. In the process, oxygen and ozone were formed, and other forms of life could be experimented with, safely screened from deadly ultraviolet light by the ozone layer. The picture is one of a remarkable interplay between the earth and its first living inhabitants, and it was a process that appears to have continued even into the present. In Louise Young's view, it is one facet of the fascinating story of the creative forces still being revealed in the natural world:

> Life altered the atmosphere and gentled the sunlight. It turned the naked rocks of the continents into friable soil and clothed them with a richly variegated mantle of green which captured the energy of our own star for the use of living things on earth, and it softened the force of the winds. In the seas life built great reefs that broke the impact of storm-driven waves. It sifted and piled up shining beaches along the shores. Working with amazing strength and endurance life transformed an ugly and barren landscape into a benign and beautiful place where wildflowers carpet the hillsides and birds embroider the air with song. The story of how all this came to pass is a shining example of the creative forces working within nature.[3]

After the first appearance of microorganisms, the evolutionary trail shows no new signs until a point 1.5 billion years ago. Again Australia provides the major clue, a set of fossils of what appears to be more complex, eukaryotic cells. It is likely that the origin of these life-forms is related to the symbiotic union of simpler organisms, in much the way that we described in the last chapter the possible union of the protein and nucleic-acid components of the early prototypes of living cells. You will recall that it had been proposed by Lynn Margolis[4] that the various organelles in a eukaryotic cell arose by symbiotic union of a host cell with bacteria having specialized attributes: bacteria with whiplike cilia for movement, those with efficient respiratory capabilities, and those with photosynthetic apparatus. With time each component of the union became more tightly integrated and more dependent upon the other. The end result was the larger eukaryotic cell with organelles specializing in inheritance (nucleus), energy (mitochondria and chloroplasts), and motion (cilia). Mitochondria were especially important because the increased concentration of oxygen raised serious problems for the oxygen-sensitive structures within cells. Even in their most primitive form, mitochondria were probably able to couple energy-forming reactions, involving the efficient oxidation of simple organic compounds, to the removal of molecular oxygen. Presumably, the original bacterial cells from which these more complex cells arose left some of their number unchanged, content to exist as before, protecting themselves from molecular oxygen by living deep in the ocean sediments. Their descendants, anaerobic bacteria and some molds and fungi, are still plentiful today and in essentially the same form they exhibited a million years ago. Their role in evolution was a relatively passive one.

Evolution toward higher levels of organization and complexity, then, was the role played by the new eukaryotic cells, and they proceeded to innovate further by experimentation with various kinds of colonial living and by sexual reproduction. Early efforts at colony formation may be illustrated by the stromatolites and coral-reef organisms, and in modern organisms is represented by the behavior of termites and bees. Sexual reproduction in primitive unicellular organisms probably occurred by way of a variation on binary fission, the usual process of reproduction in which unicellular organisms divide to produce two identical daughter cells. In rare cases it is suggested that cell division involved only one set of chromosomes, and each daughter cell was the "haploid," with only one set of the parental cells' chromosomes. When two different haploid cells met they occasionally fused to form a new individual of potentially quite different genetic makeup. The process would be slow, compared to binary fission, but the opportunity for creative change would be greatly magnified. Young[5] gives the example of an asexually reproducing species in which ten mutations occur in a given time. When these ten are subjected to natural selection, the probability of any one being favorable is very small. On the other hand, in a sexually reproducing species, the recombination of ten different mutations can produce more than a thousand variants, with much greater chance that one combination will prove beneficial.

Following the first appearance of eukaryotic cells, there is a large gap in the fossil record until about 900 million years ago, at which time fossil rocks, again in Australia, reveal a rich assemblage of unicellular organisms—algae, fungi, and other plants. Rapid evolution of eukaryotic cells had occurred, but multicellular forms had not yet appeared. Then, at a point some 700 million years ago the first traces of multicellular plants are found, fossils of green algae that have been found in both Norway and Australia. It is remarkable that the gap between the first colonies of unicellular organisms and the appearance of multicellular organisms is so large. The mechanism of evolution to multicellular organisms may have been gradual, or perhaps it occurred more suddenly by some permutation on binary fission in which two cells maintained their union, shared their information, but also retained some of their own distinctives. Colonies that assume the shape of long chains as did the primitive seaweeds and fungi may have been the ancestors of the first true multicellular plants. The advantages of the union of separate cells were many. Division of labor into specialized sets of cells led to greater efficiency. Yet these cells retained their earlier capacities and could be called upon for other functions in emergencies. There is a wholeness about self-organizing systems that is seen again here.

There is one additional fossil type that is found in geological strata dating to this period. These are the oldest multicelled animals known, and they have been found in Australia, South Africa, England, the Soviet Union, and Newfoundland. They are called the "Ediacara fauna," after the location in Australia where they were first found. Some of the fossils look as if related to later jellyfish, segmented worms, echinoderms, or corals, though most are unlike later animals.[6]

About 570 million years ago, shelled aquatic life suddenly appeared, as evidenced by extensive fossil depositions in the Burgess Shale of British Columbia. We will come back to this most important discovery, and its reinterpretation by paleontologist Stephen Gould,[7] in the next section. For the moment, it is sufficient to point out that these fauna, with soft body parts, were mysteriously unlike any that inhabited the sea subsequently. But they mysteriously disappeared from the fossil record very quickly, and were replaced by species similar to present-day snails, oysters, and sea urchins.

About 500 million years ago, aquatic animals with hard skeletons and a bone protecting a central nerve cord appeared. The most primitive fish had bony armored heads and suckers instead of movable jaws. Because of the hard body parts, the fossil record of these animals is extensive, and their number and variety have been seen to increase in a spectacular way.[8] Cephalopods, including the precursors of the present-day octopus and squid, left large numbers of fossils of often-large, funnel-shaped organisms, some more than twenty feet in length. A variety of reef-building organisms also flourished.

The upshot of this elaboration of living forms was an alteration in the biosphere as well. By 400 million years ago, the level of oxygen in the atmosphere reached present levels, and the corresponding ozone layer was adequate to confer protection from ultraviolet radiation. The stage was set for the next great step in evolution, the move to land. The transition occurred in the intertidal zone, where selective pressures were great. Plants developed strong body structures and anchoring parts as protection against the force of the waves. They developed ways to avoid desiccation and to transport moisture efficiently. Yet these adaptations are not without a certain mystery as well. The doctrine of slow alteration by chance mutation and natural selection would seem to argue for the retention of easy environments where less was demanded in order to achieve maximum survival. Yet the adaptation to land proved an enormous success, despite its more stringent requirements of body structure and nutritional requirements. Although only 30 percent of the earth's surface is land, almost 80 percent of all species are terrestrial, and these are also the most complex of the organisms that have evolved. Life seems not to follow the path of least resistance. As Louise Young puts it:

> There is something within life, within non-living matter, too, that is not passive—a nisus, a striving that is stimulated by challenge. Steadily throughout geological time life has moved out from easy to difficult environments and now has populated almost every nook and cranny of the globe, from the frozen wastes of Antarctica to the boiling sulfur-laden vents at the bottom of the sea."[9]

We are told that the first land plants left their fossil imprint at 400 million years ago. They were photosynthetic, but instead of leaves they had green porous stems for absorbing sunlight and carbon dioxide. They also had a transport system for conveying water from root hairs that gripped the soil through the thorny stalk to the upper branches. These were the pioneers of life beyond the sea. Early in this period it is likely that the symbiotic relationship between some plants and nitrogen-fixing bacteria also occurred. Nitrogen in the metabolic form of ammonia is crucial to life, but the ammonia content of the early biosphere had been depleted by reaction with oxygen as that element's concentration steadily increased. Some ammonia was probably available to plants through so-called denitri-fying bacteria, which convert nitrates generated in lightning storms to am-monia. But the larger demands of terrestrial plants would doubtless have gone unanswered without the advent of nitrogen fixation. Here, a creative association of two very different organisms occurred. The nitrogen-fixing organism is a very primitive anaerobic bacterium, necessarily parasitic be-cause it never developed a full metabolic capability, and extremely sensitive to oxygen. But it had one extraordinary feature, an enzyme system called nitrogenase, which was capable of reducing atmospheric nitrogen to am-monia. Present-day organisms of this type are still totally dependent for their metabolic needs upon their plant host. They cannot metabolize nor can they fix nitrogen in the absence of the symbiotic relationship. They are, of course, of tremendous importance to present-day agriculture, where they are found in association with the root nodules of the legumes—peas, beans, and clover.

Young tells us that the first land animals were found as fossils dating to about 390 million years ago.[10] They were spiderlike and air-breathing, and they were followed 30 million years later by an air-breathing fish that also had bony fins that presumably provided for movement on land. We do not know what led these creatures onto the land, though it is suggested that, once there, a strong drive for self-preservation was apparent. Each step in the building process toward more advanced levels of form had to be retained. Self-preservation is a universal phenomenon.

The rest of the story of biological evolution is perhaps more familiar to us, though hardly any less amazing in its creativity and scope. Within the animals, the number of phyla—the largest subdivisions of the organisms of the animal kingdom, based upon each possessing a fundamentally distinct body plan, has been designated as thirty-two.[11,12] These include sponges, corals (including hydras and jellyfish), annelids (earthworms, leeches, and polychaetes), arthropods (insects, spiders, lobsters, and their relatives), mollusks (clams, snails, squid), echinoderms (starfishes, sea urchins, and sand dollars), and chordates (vertebrates and their kin). Also included as separate phyla are the comb jellies, flatworms, bivalved invertebrates, and nematodes. All told, most modern textbooks recognize between twenty and thirty animal phyla. All these modern organisms have come to us by this amazing evolutionary path—itself tortuous, devious, full of pitfalls and dead ends, festooned with the successful and littered with the debris of the unsuccessful. Self-preservation may be a universal drive, but is not always sufficient. The dinosaurs may have had the best intentions, but the huge comet that apparently struck the earth 65 million years ago left them no choice—they all perished. But their demise opened the way for mammals including ourselves.

One further development deserves mention in this brief look at the later stages of life's evolution. Anthropologist Loren Eiseley tells us in the *Immense Journey*[13] that the end of the age of the dinosaurs also marked the emergence of the angiosperms—the flowering plants. It was an explosive development, by evolutionary standards, for within a few million years the entire face of the planet changed, and with it came the high-energy food sources necessary to the life of warm-blooded animals. The explosive appearance of the angiosperms even troubled Charles Darwin, who called them an "abominable mystery" because of their sudden appearance and rapid dissemination.

The animals that lived in the age of the dinosaurs were lumbering, slow-moving, slow-thinking creatures that moved about in the warmth of day but lay torpid on chill nights. They were cold-blooded, and the temperature of their world determined their activity. They were slaves to the weather.

The warm-blooded animals that followed the disappearance of the dinosaurs had a higher metabolic rate and were able to maintain a constant body temperature. Eiseley refers to these as supreme achievements in the evolution of life.[14] They provided for freedom of the animal from overheating and chilling while at the same time maintaining a peak mental efficiency. However, a high metabolic rate implies a need for large amounts of energy. The agile brain of the warm-blooded birds and mammals demanded high oxygen consumption and concentrated foods. It was the flowering plants that met that need. Their appearance parallels in a striking manner the rise of birds and mammals.

The earlier plants reproduced by means of microscopic swimming sperm that traveled through the water to reach and fertilize the female cell. With the advent of the first primitive flowering plant, the sperm traveled instead as pollen grains, disseminated by wind and insect, and the march across dry land began. Instead of spores, simple primitive seeds developed, probably first in the wooden coneflowers of the pine and spruce forests. These developments paralleled the events of animal evolution. The egg of a fish is deposited and fertilized in the water whereas the mammalian fertilized cell is carefully retained by its mother until the young has developed sufficiently to make survival more feasible. Similarly, the angiosperm grows a seed in the heart of a flower, fertilizes it with a pollen grain, nurtures the fully equipped embryonic plant, and prepares it for dissemination. The thistle attaches down to its seed to catch the wind, the burdock a hook to catch a passing animal, and many others an enticing fruit to be carried away. Most importantly, these seeds and fruits represented the kind of concentrated nourishment needed by the warm-blooded birds and mammals.

The amount of speciation that occurred in this period was also striking. The primitive grasses that covered the earth in all kinds of habitats rapidly diverged and have now become six thousand modern species. The amount of innovation among the animals also increased greatly. Specialized groups of insects arose to feed on the new food sources, and incidentally to pollinate the plants. As Eiseley says it so very well:

> Intricate mechanisms splashed pollen on the breasts of hummingbirds, or stamped it on the bellies of black, grumbling bees droning assiduously from blossom to blossom. Honey ran, insects multiplied, and even the descendants of that toothed and ancient lizard-bird had become strangely altered. Equipped with prodding beaks instead of biting teeth, they pecked the seeds and gobbled the insects that were really converted nectar.[15]

One cannot view such marvelously coincident phenomena as flowers and warm-blooded creatures without realizing that all of nature displays a connectedness, an exquisite interlinkage. Flowers did indeed change the face of the planet. The English poet, Francis Thompson, once wrote that one could not pluck a flower without troubling a star. Again, in Eiseley's words:

> Without the gift of flowers and the infinite diversity of their fruit, man and bird, if they had continued to exist at all, would be today unrecognizable. Archaeopteryx, the lizard-bird, might still be snapping at beetles on a sequoia limb; man might still be a nocturnal insectivore gnawing a roach in the dark. The weight of a petal has changed the face of the world and made it ours.[16]

III. Discontinuities in Biological Evolution

The general picture of evolutionary development of living things seems secure, but there are some remarkable discontinuities, some of which we have already mentioned, which preclude any simple explanation. Indeed, life arose and developed by some rather remarkable and highly improbable steps. In fact, some of the gaps in this developmental picture are so enormous—such as the billion years that elapsed between unicellular and multicellular life—that talk of the inevitability of life as we know it seems ridiculous to many biologists.

Such is the stance of paleontologist Stephen Gould, whom we mentioned earlier in this chapter as a reinterpreter of the data of the Burgess Shale.[17] Gould's thesis is that the developments of the Cambrian period, 570 million years ago, when the first multicellular animals suddenly appear in great profusion, represents the most important story of biological evolution. The "Cambrian explosion" represents the advent of virtually all major groups of modern animals, and within the brief period—geologically speaking—of a few million years. The unique place of the Burgess Shale, a block-long slab of rock in British Columbia, is that the fossils they contain preserve in exquisite detail, even to the last meal in a worm's gut, the soft anatomy of organisms. Recall that hard parts are those generally preserved as fossils. The first animals had none so the unique depositions in the Burgess Shale are, in Gould's words, "precious windows into the true range and diversity of ancient life." [18]

The Burgess Shale's fossils were discovered in 1909 by the American paleontologist Charles Walcott of the Smithsonian Institution, and were interpreted erroneously within the established paradigm of evolution. In Gould's words, "he shoehorned every last Burgess animal into a modern group, viewing the fauna collectively as a set of primitive or ancestral versions of later, improved forms."

By contrast, the 1971 reinterpretation of the Burgess organisms by Harry Wittington of Cambridge University, with which Gould concurs, places the Burgess fossils in an astoundingly different light. Most of the Burgess organisms do not belong to familiar groups, and the anatomical variety far exceeds the modern range. What appears to be the case is that tremendous creativity occurred in the Cambrian period, but only a few of these novel creatures have evolved to be part of the smaller group of modern animal types. The history given by the Burgess Shale is one of a creative explosion followed by massive extinction of almost all the representatives of that experimentation.

As Gould describes it:

> The creatures from this single quarry in British Columbia probably exceed, in anatomical range, the entire spectrum of invertebrate life in today's oceans. Some fifteen to twenty Burgess species cannot be allied with any known group, and should probably be classified as separate phyla. Magnify some of them beyond the few centimeters of their actual size, and you are on the set of a science-fiction film; one particularly arresting creature has been formally named *Hallucigenia*. For species that can be classified within known phyla, Burgess anatomy far exceeds the modern range. The

Burgess Shale includes, for example, early representatives of all four major kinds of arthropods, the dominant animals on earth today—the trilobites (now extinct), the crustaceans (including lobsters, crabs, and shrimp), the chelicerates (including spiders and scorpions), and the uniramians (including insects). But the Burgess Shale also contains some twenty to thirty kinds of arthropods that cannot be placed in any modern group. Consider the magnitude of this difference: taxonomists have described almost a million species of arthropods, and all fit into four major groups; one quarry in British Columbia, representing the first explosion of multicellular life, reveals more than twenty additional arthropod designs! The history of life is a story of massive removal followed by differentiation within a few surviving stocks, not the conventional tale of steadily increasing excellence, complexity, and diversity.[19]

Gould recognizes that one of the problems posed by the modern interpretation of the Burgess Shale is the question of the source of the variety or disparity and the speed of its appearance.[20] One explanation relates to the setting in which the Burgess fauna developed. It is noted that there was little competition, and so organisms were free to experiment, with little selection pressure to sort out less adapted forms. Gould's rebuttal is that no such explosion of new organisms occurred after the Permian extinction, which occurred some 225 million years ago, when 96 percent of marine species disappeared from the fossil record. If ecological opportunity was all that involved, then a tremendous increase in disparity should have been seen in the next geologic era, the Mesozoic, but it is not evident. What he suggests as an alternative is that the tremendous outburst of variety of organisms in the Cambrian and the later quiescence is due to change in organic potential.[21] The idea that organisms may play active roles in determining their direction of evolutionary change has gained popularity with recent advances in our understanding of genetic systems. J. W. Valentine has suggested that genetic systems may actually "age" in the sense of becoming "less forgiving of major restructuring." [22] Perhaps there are internal reasons for modern organisms to be resistant to originating an array of new designs in the way the Burgess fauna arose. Perhaps the genomes of the latter were simpler and more flexible. It is also possible that the presence of multiple copies of genes in more modern organisms provides an interlocking web of interactions that preclude rearrangement.

Gould goes on to explain that the conventional argument usually offered for the rapid disappearance of the Burgess fauna is that the majority of the phyla were faulty—the majority of experiments did not work. Does it really matter if only a few of the perhaps hundreds of possibilities were well enough adapted to survive? Those were the few that would have proved successful in any case, for they were "the root stocks for all later life no matter how many times we replayed the tape." [23] The problem with this view, Gould says, is that the design of the Burgess fauna is not seen to be inferior. Modern interpreters of the Burgess organisms have concluded that they demonstrate anatomical integrity and efficient feeding and locomotion. The more they looked at the "losers,'" the more they realized that we do not know why some of the organisms succeeded and some did not. Gould suggests that the Burgess decimation, the loss of those many grand designs, may have been a true lottery. If the tape could be replayed, there would be a new set of winners, and, by extrapolation, we probably would not be here! To Gould this is not a dim prospect but rather a liberation.

In Gould's words,

> If we could wind the tape of life back to the Burgess, why should we not have a different set of winners on a replay? Perhaps, this time, all surviving lineages would be locked into a developmental pattern of biramous limbs, well suited for life in the water but not for successful invasion of the land. Perhaps, therefore, this alternative world would have no cockroaches, no mosquitoes, and no black flies—but also no bees and ultimately, no pretty flowers.

> Extend this theme beyond arthropods to the weird wonders of the Burgess. Why not *Opabinia* and *Wiwaxia*? Why not a world of grazing marine herbivores bearing sclerites, not snail shells? Why not *Anomalocaris* and a world of marine predators with grasping limbs up front and a jaw like a nutcracker?...

> The idea of decimation as a lottery converts the new iconography of the Burgess Shale into a radical view about the pathways of life and the nature of history. I dedicate this book to exploring the consequences of this view. May our poor and improbable species find joy in its new-found fragility and good fortune! Wouldn't anyone with the slightest sense of adventure, or the most weakly flickering respect for intellect, gladly exchange the old cosmic comfort for a look at something so weird and wonderful—yet so real—as *Opabinia?* [24]

Of course it remains to be seen just how crucial the Burgess Shale story is to the whole picture of biological evolution. One is tempted to suggest that there is more of the zeal of the evangelist in Gould's story than seems appropriate. And the focus on one part—albeit surely a fascinating part—of the evolution story we have been considering largely ignores major aspects such as cooperative interaction between organism and environment and of symbiosis between organisms. These factors loom large in any picture of biological evolution though they too are uncertain and somewhat hypothetical. What seems indisputable is that complexity has increased with the evolution of simple unicellular systems to multicellular and from the relatively simple organisms of the Cambrian to the higher primates and finally to human consciousness. Perhaps Gould is right in his belief that that sequence would never replay again. We do not think present data or even the trend in the data demands that conclusion. We might or might not be in the replay.

But we *are* in the play! And it is an astounding scenario.

IV. The Character of Life

Louise Young has presented the idea of a universe in a state of genesis, in dynamic motion, where states of being are only single frames in the motion picture of life. In fact, what we have is a universal process of evolving form—form set free to dance. Everything is in a state of transition in one direction, toward more complex, more highly integrated form. Molecules, organisms, species are not fixed states of being but stages of becoming. "Becoming," Young says, "stands forth as the essential reality." [25]

The question of the huge gap between the appearance of unicellular forms and the advent of multicellular life is explainable in terms of the experimentation with new forms. Such experimentation is readily visible in the modern biosphere, where a large middle ground exists that is occupied by living things that are neither wholly unicellular of wholly multicellular. For example, many species of algae, protozoa, fungi, and bacteria are colonial for part of their life cycles. The classic example is the slime mold, *Dictyostelium discoideum*. Its early life is as an amoeba-like soil organism, feeding on bacteria, and reproducing by binary fission. Under conditions of food shortage, growth stops and cells converge to form a conical mound that can become a long stalk with spores at the top and a supporting disk at the base. The spores are then disseminated and the structure disintegrates. In this differentiation process, one type of cell becomes three, the choice of which type depending upon the place each cell takes in the aggregate. As few as ten cells can provide the chemical signals and interactions needed to carry out this reproductive phase.

A second example of modern life forms at the borderline between the individual cell and the colonial state is provided by the sponge. This animal has a tubular structure with many pores lined with tiny cells called collar cells that flail threadlike whips to move water in the desired direction of flow. There are also several types of cells that compose the skin, the middle layer, and the skeleton of the sponge. Many years ago a biologist named H. V. Wilson experimented with sponge organization by mincing entire sponges into individual cells and small aggregates of cells. The cells now behaved like amoebae, extending lobes and moving along the surface. But soon a remarkable thing happened. When cells touched they joined and gradually a mass of cells was formed. These cellular masses then joined with each other to form a single mass that finally differentiated into the four types of cells of the sponge. The tubular structure was constructed; the skeleton, the middle body, and the skin. It is said that the biologist, Edmund Sinnott, commenting on this experiment, said

> In some way the structure of the whole sponge, with its specific pattern and its cellular activity, is immanent in each individual cell. How this is possible is a secret still locked in the innermost structure of protoplasm. Evidently each tiny living unit is a much more complex thing than it appears to be, for it bears within itself an image of the whole organism.[26]

There are many other examples of closely cooperative relationships. The honeybee, for example, is the apex of cooperative insect societies, and the lichen is a double plant consisting of a moldlike fungus and a single-celled algae in symbiotic union. Indeed, there are many different levels of internally organized systems that display cooperative relationships. These intermediate systems, in which the distinction between individual species seems to be blurred, appear everywhere. As Young says:

> When we think of the living world in terms of discrete forms and species, we are focusing on certain stages of the transformation process. The many intermediate systems appear to be anomalies that do not fit conveniently into any one category. But when we think in terms of continuous change moving toward the formation of more complex self-regulating wholes, the intermediate states fall into place as essential parts of the process.[27]

This idea of the evolution of form toward complexity in terms of cooperative relationships has deep significance for our understanding of our world and ourselves. There may be an even larger organization of matter, the earth itself, which takes on at times the appearance of a living creature. Physician-writer Lewis Thomas once commented:

> Viewed from the distance of the moon, the astonishing thing about the earth, catching the breath, is that it is alive. The photographs show the dry, pounded surface of the moon in the foreground, dead as an old bone. Aloft, floating free beneath the moist, gleaming membrane of bright blue sky, is the rising earth, the only exuberant thing in this part of the cosmos. If you could look long enough, you would see the swirling of the great drifts of white cloud, covering and uncovering the half-hidden masses of land. If you had been looking for a very long geological time, you could have seen the continents themselves in motion, drifting apart on their crustal plates, held afloat by the fire beneath. It has the organized, self-

contained look of a live creature, full of information, marvelously skilled in handling the sun.[28]

This idea had been greatly extended by British scientist James Lovelock, who had given the name Gaia to an interpretation of the earth as a self-regulating system that provides the appropriate conditions for life.[29] As evidence for this view he cites the unique and improbable combination of gases in the atmosphere, extremely favorable for life, which have been maintained within very narrow limits for a long period of time. So also the composition of the oceans, which geological data suggests has been held at a 3.4 percent salt concentration for at least a hundred million years. Finally, the climate of the earth has been amazingly uniform since life first appeared. These facts could be just a series of lucky circumstances, but the more likely explanation is that the biosphere is a self-regulating system that is actively manipulating the environment and maintaining the conditions most favorable for its own existence.

Evolution is a much more mysterious and complex phenomenon than the paradigm of gradual change with time might suggest. Indeed, improbable arrangements of matter and energy seem to be the rule, and these all appear to be in dynamic flux, moving toward higher complexity and more intricate and holistic relationships as time passes. In fact, the term *evolution* means to unfold, like the opening of a flower bud or even the reading out of a predetermined plan. Young thinks this meaning is unfortunate, since it is obvious that the design has been faulty, with many imperfections and failures and extinctions along with the many great breakthroughs in creative novelty. If the universe was intended to lead to absolute beauty and goodness, the design would seem poor indeed. However, if the process actually depends upon trial and error, then imperfection and failure are necessary features. But Young concludes: "The existence of tragic mistakes would not be expected at all if a pattern, already created, were simply being unrolled."[30]

Indeed, these tragic mistakes and discontinuities have made other biologists reluctant even to assign a direction to biological evolution. The choice of one organism as "more advanced" than another is often difficult. Primitive anaerobic bacteria, to take an extreme case, are said to be as well adapted to their environment as human beings are to ours. Julian Huxley once addressed this question as follows:

> It is...an empirical fact that evolutionary progress can only be measured by the upper level reached, for the lower levels are also retained. The retention of lower levels has on numerous occasions been used as an argument against the existence of anything which can properly be called progress: but its employment in this connection is fallacious. It is on a par

with saying that the invention of the automobile does not represent an advance, because horse-drawn vehicles remain more convenient for certain purposes, or pack animals for certain localities.... We can discern a direction—the line of evolutionary progress: increase of control, increase of independence, increase of internal coordination; increase of knowledge, of means for coordinating knowledge, of elaborateness and intensity of feeling—those are trends of the most general order.[31]

To this statement Louise Young adds:

The classic argument about the reality of evolutionary progress can be seen as a problem in semantics. If one defines progress as the degree of improvement in adaptation to the environment then some of the very simplest organisms meet this test as well as more conplex ones. But if one assumes with Huxley that evolutionary progress is measured by improvement in internal organization, in greater control, independence, and potential, then the changes that have occurred throughout time have produced spectacular advances as complexity has increased from the simple one-celled organism without nucleus or organelles to the human being containing as many as a hundred trillion eukaryotic cells.[32]

V. The Theology of Biological Evolution

Our current understanding of the evolution of life poses important questions for any theological view of creation. A God who is intimately involved in the processes of evolution would seem to have some purpose other than the unfolding of a perfect predetermined plan. As we have said, the path of evolution is strewn with failed experiments, with enormous periods of time when little seemed to be happening and with many promising paths that nevertheless ended in extinction. And, too, some of the most intricate of cooperative behaviors, such as the shift of the slime mold *Dictyostelium discoideum* from a single-celled phase to a reproductive phase, begins with an apparent random choice of one cell to be the focal point for aggregation. Chance appears to be an intrinsic part of our universe.

Recall that this was also the case in chapter 4 where we reviewed the arguments for a second arrow of time, an optimistic arrow that points in the direction of ever-increasing complexity and diversity of form. The drive toward new order, novelty, and complexity is related to newly discovered chemical processes that occur under nonlinear, far-from-equilibrium conditions and often display chaotic behavior. These are the predominant form of chemical reactions in nature, and they are most interesting for our present discussion because they are unpredictable and far more error-prone than linear systems and yet at the same time demonstrate the capacity for spontaneous self-organization.

Somehow the interplay of randomness and orderliness is a key in the self-organization of the universe. Physicist-theologian John Polkinghorne, in his book *Science and Creation*,[33] points out that the most fruitful relationship between randomness and order is provided by the insight that it is the interplay of chance and necessity that characterizes the evolution of the universe and of life. Polkinghorne is quick to point out that the significance of the existence of chance has been widely debated. Molecular biologist Jacques Monod argued in his book, *Chance and Necessity*, that the role of chance is evidence of meaninglessness in the process of the world. He says "pure chance, absolutely free but blind, [is] at the very root of the stupendous edifice of evolution," and concludes that "the ancient covenant is in pieces; man at last knows that he is alone in the unfeeling vastness of the universe, out of which he emerged by chance. Neither his destiny nor his duty have been written down."[34]

However, to Polkinghorne, the role of chance is to exhibit the potentiality inherent in the properties of matter and is "so remarkable as to constitute an insight of design present in the structure of the world."[35] Elsewhere, he has written:

> When I read Monod's book I was greatly excited by the scientific picture it presented of how life came to be. As a particle physicist, I found the biochemical details pretty difficult to follow but, assuming them to be correct, they implied that Schrödinger's equation and Maxwell's equations (the fundamental dynamical equations of quantum theory and electromagnetism respectively, which I could literally write down on the back of an envelope) had this astonishing consequence of the emergence of replicating molecules and eventually life. The economy and profundity of that is breathtaking. For me, the beauty that it revealed in the structure of the world was like a rehabilitation of the argument from design—not as a knockdown argument for the existence of God (there are no such arguments; nor are there for his non-existence) but as an insight into the way the world is."[36]

What Polkinghorne concludes is that chance in this context is the occurrence of a chain of uncorrelated possibilities, providing the raw material for novelty and innovation. This raw material is then explored by the intervention of lawful necessity—by the selective mechanisms of nature at various levels—and those configurations are preserved that prove fruitful for survival and replication.

This kind of world displays orderliness but not clockwork regularity, "potentiality without predictability, endowed with an assurance of development but with a certain openness as to its actual form."[37] Such a world cannot avoid having ragged edges where, side by side with the production of new forms and potentialities, will occur imperfections and dysfunctions. The world we live in with physical evils such as earthquakes and epidemics reflects "the untidiness of disorder" just as the rich variety and beauty of nature reflects "the organizing power of order. Each is the inescapable complement of the other." [38]

Here then is a hint that the phenomena of order and disorder are somehow bound up with an explanation for the Creator's activity in the universe. Theology appears to establish that the world is a creation, so that its process could be the expression of the Creator's intentions. Theology seems to imply too that the Creator is both good and all-powerful, the latter implying that the Creator may freely express his will. No world of Platonic forms imposes on him an obligatory order nor is there a force of evil strong enough to thwart his purpose. This is the external freedom of God. No external agency limits his power or rejects his will. But there are internal constraints. For God is not a pompous dictator exercising his sovereignty in an arbitrary manner. He is internally constrained by the consistency of his own character. As omnipotent Creator he can do what he wills, but only in accord with his own character. Among these constraints, Polkinghorne includes God's respect for reason. He will not decree that $2 + 2 = 5$. And he is not an arbitrary intervener in the processes of the world. Such intervention must again be consistent with his character. And so the laws of nature are evidence of his fidelity—his faithfulness. God is also love, and this necessitates that he grant freedom generously, for "love is grounded in the free interchange between lover and beloved." [39]

The balance between these internal restraints is delicate. Faithfulness is expressed as order, but love gives freedom that opens up the possibility for disorder. And so the universe and all of its parts, as the free creation of God, may be expected to be open to chance at the same time that it displays the regularity of natural law; chance and necessity operating in appropriate proportion to fulfill the Creator's will. Here there is, according to Polkinghorne, no room for the idea that God is some kind of demiurge struggling to maintain control or to arrange fruitful coincidence. Yet, if the world is contingent, in some sense free and unpredictable, then the Creator must also by flexible and temporal. However, the Creator has also made a remarkably intelligible world, rational and consistent, and this seems to require of God's nature that it be immutable and eternal. As Polkinghorne puts it, "God's internal complexity is such that he can embrace both the necessary and the contingent, the eternal and the temporal. This divine complementarity of being and becoming is the theological counterpart of the chance and necessity that the scientist discerns in the process of the world." [40]

Polkinghorne goes on to emphasize a crucial theological idea, that "the act of creation involves a *kinosis* of God, an emptying of himself and an acceptance of the self-limitation inherent in the giving of creative love.... There is a vulnerability involved in creation which God freely embraces."[41]

Then he goes on to quote from theologian W. H. Vanstone:

> The activity of God in creation must be precarious. It must proceed by no assured program. Its progress, like every progress of love, must be an angular progress—in which each step is a precarious step into the unknown....
> If the creation is the work of love, then its shape cannot be predetermined by the Creator, nor its triumph foreknown: it is the realization of vision, but of vision which is discovered only through its own realization: all faith in its triumph is neither more or less than faith in the Creator Himself— faith that He will not cease from His handiwork nor abandon the object of His love.[42]

Polkinghorne calls this view of the creator God the divine Juggler rather than the divine Structural Engineer, exploring the universe's inherent potentiality through the trial-and-error methods of chance, being pleased and successful in ways not foreseen, and realizing a vision only discovered through its own realization.

Perhaps God could be called the divine Experimenter.

VI. Reality

Earlier we talked about the possibility of "becoming" as the essential reality. The universe is in process, striving for higher form in one grand, concerted, mysterious march. Now in addressing the evolutionary process, it seems to us that the idea of becoming assumes an even deeper reality. Behind the physical insight of a universe exploring its potentiality is a God who is both the ground of order and the provider of freedom of choice of contingent events. He is both God of necessity and God of chance—both reliable and vulnerable.

The universe is not only greater in magnitude and intricacy than we had dreamed, but it is willed into being at every moment by a divine plan that is both faithful and loving. This is the deeper meaning of being and becoming. Perhaps it is not only the essential—but the only—reality.

Summary

Evolutionary theory has undergone a remarkable metamorphosis in the past few decades. Instead of the earlier picture of the *gradual* change of form toward complexity, the data demonstrate that whole new groups of organisms have "exploded" into view in many parts of the fossil record.

Furthermore, events have occurred with such exquisite timing that it is even tempting to invoke some grand homeostatic mechanism for the whole process. Certainly, a high order of opportunism is in view, with new cooperative relationships appearing everywhere.

In any case, evolutionary science appears far more uncertain and mysterious than just a few decades ago. Again, we see the goal of fully grasping reality through science as a fleeting one. Reality is deeper than we are.

The definition of Reality in terms of the faithful and loving God of the universe—the divine Experimenter—seems to us a far more profound and powerful explanation.

7

Self-Organization and the Evolution of Humankind

I. Cultural Aspects of the Study of Human Evolution

When we look at the creative paradigm from the standpoint of our own origin, the exploration reveals not only a fascinating trail of surprises—especially in the past few decades—but also brings with it a recognition of the complexity of the human equation. For here in the evolution of man, we are confronted by profound cultural components that enter into the rate of evolutionary change and also profoundly shape the way we interpret the biological data.

Roger Lewin, in his book *In the Age of Mankind*[1] points out that paleoanthropology, the search for human origins, carries with it the same characteristics as any science; the temporary nature of theory, based upon mental constructs that are subject to revised perceptions of existing and new data. And because science is done by people, not automatons, it also carries the probability of personal biases and even capricious interpretation. But paleoanthropology is especially sensitive in these personal dimensions, because it attempts to explain the origin and place of *Homo sapiens* in nature. It therefore carries with it a higher degree of emotionalism and social overlay than one might find in the study of say, parasitic flatworms. As Lewin says: "What has for millennia been the object of the origin myths cannot readily—if at all—be stripped of subjective social content, even if that were desirable."[2]

Yet this extrascientific component is not viewed by all anthropologists as inappropriate. Duke University anthropologist Matt Cartmill has responded to criticisms of what he calls the "mythological content" in anthropology with the argument that the inclusion of the mythological gives a more complete description and makes paleoanthropology "more, not less than scientific." And he adds: "The mythic dimension is plus, not instead of. The theories still have to resist attempts to prove them false, but they don't *mean* as much without those extensions into the extra-scientific."[3]

Much of what is written about human origins is colored by our fascination with the question of our own meaning. Who are we? What are we? Surely, we are different from the rest of the biological world. Evolutionary biologist David Wilcox of Eastern College has pointed out that there appears to be no nonhuman equivalent to abstract reasoning, representational art, contextual linguistic structure, religious belief, accumulated knowledge, or cultural flexibility and complexity. Yet this sense of our uniqueness is often questioned by the more material-minded, who find human meanings and relationships in other creatures and by all of us as we project our own image across the whole spectrum of reality.[4] Perhaps, materialists say, the theist's belief in a personal God is only another kind of projection. Yet theists note that, as Boston University anthropologist Misia Landau suggests, materialists have often been guilty of a rather nonmaterial view of human origins as the inevitable progress of the hero, the apelike creature who undertakes a tortuous journey, leaving the safety of the trees for the grassy savanna and through ice ages and other hazards finally reaches a state of human civilization.[5] We are all storytellers!

Except perhaps for Stephen J. Gould, who you will recall from the last chapter charged Charles Walcott with a disastrous misinterpretation of the Burgess Shale. Indeed, Gould decries the extent to which concept affects scientific work, and makes a plea for a careful reading of history in our understanding of evolution. His rather amazing conclusion to the Walcott analysis is:

> I know no finer illustration of the most important message taught by the history of science: the subtle and inevitable hold that theory exerts upon data and observation. Reality does not speak to us objectively, and no scientist can be free from constraints of psyche and society. The greatest impediment to scientific innovation is usually a conceptual lock, not a factual lack....The new view of the Burgess Shale is no more nor less than the triumph of history itself as a favored principle for reading the evolution of life.[6]

The salient view of the history of evolution in Gould's eyes is un-repeatability. If the tape were to be rewound and replayed, the picture would be totally different. There is no *one* story, no single interpretation. We are an accident of history. But if there is no one story, is that not also a story! If man is the product of forces that did not have him in mind, is that not also a concept—and possibly a conceptual lock?

II. The Biology of Human Evolution

A. THE MOLECULAR CLOCK

Until relatively recently, the nearest lineage to the human family was be-lieved to be represented by a fossil of a fifteen-million-year-old ape called *Ramapithecus*. However, in the 1960s a series of biochemical studies were carried out by Morris Goodman of Wayne State University and Allan Wilson and Vincent Sarich of the University of California that compared the blood proteins of the great apes—the chimpanzee, the gorilla, and the orangutan—and humans.[7] Until this time, anthropologists had included all the great apes in one family, Pongidae, and the humans in a second family, Hominidae. What the comparison of their various blood proteins revealed was that the orangutan was the odd species, whereas the other apes *and* humans were very closely related. This conclusion was based upon mea-surements of the molecular clock, which depends upon the gradual roughly clocklike accumulation of changes in protein structure that are a reflection of slowly accumulated changes in the DNA coding for those proteins. Now if one imagines a common ancestor that gives rise to the ape and human lineages, and establishes a rate at which the blood protein changes occur as a function of time, then the differences can be interpreted as a measure of the time since the lineages separated. More recently, Wilson and Sarich have carried out many more experiments, measuring a variety of proteins and the DNA itself and these have all supported a close relationship be-tween African apes and humans, with a date for the separation of the two lineages at between four and eight million years age. The gorilla lineage was the first to split sway, perhaps five million years ago. All of this, though slowly and grudgingly accepted by paleoanthropologists, supports a sur-prisingly recent and intimate relationship between the African ape stock and the human lineage.

B. THE EARLIEST HOMINIDS

Six decades ago the scientific world was astounded by the discovery in a South African limestone quarry called the Taung Cave, of a small skull that was proposed to be that of an upright-walking "manlike" ape that lived one to two million years ago.[8] The discoverer, anatomist Raymond Dart, of the University of the Witwatersrand of South Africa, called the creature *Australopithicus africanus* or southern ape of Africa. Laymen dubbed it the Taung child. Dart's evidence consisted of a partial cranium, the face and lower jaw of a child estimated to be six years of age. The shape of the cranium and the way it connected to the spinal column indicated that the individual walked erect, unlike any modern ape. It also lacked the larger canine teeth of modern apes. Most importantly, a limestone cast of the brain cavity was also found, and this demonstrated to the trained anatomist a mini-topography that was much more human than apelike.

But to the scientific world, the proposal that there was an African ape-man was astounding, especially since almost nothing was known then of small-brained hominids who walked erect. And Africa was certainly not the place where anthropologists had expected to see the precursors of mankind. Indeed the important hominid fossils up to that time, with the exception of Piltdown man, were Asian. Numerous remnants of Java man had been found, beginning in the 1890s, and Peking man in the 1920s. An Asian or at least Near Eastern origin for mankind seemed more likely and appropriate. As for Piltdown, it, too, served to bias anthropologists, toward a large-brained early progenitor of modern humans. In Weaver's words:

> In truth, Dart's missing link was anatomically inconvenient, with its small brain, low forehead, and small humanlike lower jaw. According to the prevailing idea of the day, primitive man should have had a big brain and an apelike jaw with big front teeth. And to prove it, Britain had its famous Piltdown skull, discovered in 1911, with a high forehead, big brain, and large canine tooth. Dart's detractors could not know that within thirty years Piltdown man would be proved a fake. To this day no one is sure who perpetrated this gigantic hoax by salting a modern human skull with a doctored-up orangutan jaw in deposits in southeastern England.[9]

It was also a surprise to the anthropology world when, six years after Dart's discovery, anthropologist Louis Leakey proclaimed that he was going to Africa in search of ancient man, whom he believed had his origin there but was unrelated to the *Australopithecus* genus. Leakey, the son of British missionaries to Kenya, chose the Olduvai Gorge in northern Tanzania for his first explorations . Olduvai is a twenty-five-mile-long river-carved canyon some three hundred feet deep that drops abruptly into the Serengeti Plain. It is part of the Great Rift Valley, a gigantic rupture in the earth's surface that runs all the way from the Gulf of Aden through eastern Africa and on into southern Africa. Faulting, upthrust, and erosion have exposed lake and river sediments and a wealth of fossils at various depths.[10] At Olduvai, the lowest levels date back two million years.

Louis Leakey and his archaeologist wife Mary spent over fifty years together detailing the record of human prehistory at Olduvai.[11] What they found first were large numbers of primitive stone tools. However, the first hominid skull was only found there in 1959. The story goes that one morning, while Louis lay in bed in his tent ill with a fever, Mary decided to explore one of the gullies tributary to the main gorge. Searching for telltale pieces of bone, she suddenly saw two huge teeth and a piece of skull. With great excitement she scurried back to camp shouting "I've got him! I've got him!" The Leakeys returned with dental tools and fine brushes and eventually sieved out some four hundred fragments with which to reconstruct a skull that would have held a brain 530 milliliters in size. The face and cheek teeth were massive, so much so that he came to be known as Nutcracker man. He was called "Zinjanthropus," or East African man, and was proclaimed by the Leakeys to be man's direct ancestor. Later evidence convinced the Leakeys that Zinjanthropus was not the direct line to modern humans but was instead another australopithecine related to those discovered by Raymond Dart, but with heavier bone structure. Along with Scottish physician Robert Broom, Dart had described a number of australopithecinelike individuals with heavier teeth and lower jaw that have now been classified as *Australopithecus robustus*. Leakey called his Zinjanthropus *Australopithecus boisei*, considering it sufficiently different from *A. robustus* to deserve its own name.[12]

Despite the slow progress, there were decided advantages to the diggings that the Leakeys began at Olduvai, since the strata are interwoven with many layers of tuff, or hardened volcanic ash, allowing for more accurate dating and cross-comparison of fossils. Each layer of tuff is unique to a given volcanic event and carries its own unique chemical fingerprint. By using a radiometric dating technique, the decay of radioactive potassium to argon, the tuff layer at the lowest level at Olduvai, where hominid fossils were later found, was dated at 1.8 million years. This particular measurement, made in 1961, suggested that the time span of human evolution was destined to be radically lengthened.

Indeed, the year after Mary Leakey discovered Zinjanthropus, the Leakeys found a much more likely candidate for human ancestry. What they uncovered, in the lowest layer of the canyon, were parts of the cranium, jaw, and hand of a more slightly built creature with a larger brain than Zinjanthropus. It was christened *Homo habilis*, or Handy man, and it has been generally accepted as the first known representative of our own genus.

Further examples of early hominids were subsequently found at Lake Turkana in northern Kenya by Richard Leakey, son of Louis and Mary. In fact, during the first ten years of the Lake Turkana explorations, the remains of over two hundred hominid individuals, including some twenty complete or almost complete skulls, had been discovered. Many of the fossils were like Zinjanthropus, and so were classified australopithecines. Many others were more slightly built and appeared to be fossils of *Homo habilis*. And there were some individuals that were enigmatic, and seemed to beg for some new classification. But the general impression that seemed to be emerging from the Lake Turkana fossils was that two million years ago there were two main branches to the human family tree; *Homo*, which eventually led to modern humans, and *Australopithecus*, which eventually *became extinct*. And the Leakeys believed that the two lines went back more than five million years.

And then came the discovery of the truly ancient hominid Lucy by Donald Johanson in north central Ethiopia in 1974.[13] Johanson went to the Hadar region of Ethiopia as coleader of an American/French expedition. It was a great opportunity for a young anthropologist just finishing his doctorate, and he took full advantage of it. The region had been selected by French geologist Maurice Taleb as a likely spot for fossil hunting. It too was in the Great Rift Valley, at its northern extremity, and was once the location of a great lake, an ideal site for fossilization. On one occasion Johanson and a colleague were searching one of the parched gullies of the Afar badlands when he spotted a piece of bone on the eroded slope above them. The fossil had probably been exposed by one of the flash floods that on rare occasions cut through the gullies. It was a piece of an arm bone, and it was hominid! Johanson recalls his astonishment with the words, "This thing was just so incredibly primitive. When I saw the armbone I thought it was a monkey's." No sooner had he changed his interpretation than they spied another bone—part of a skull. And then the slope just sprouted fossils—here a thighbone, there vertebrae and ribs, farther up a section of pelvis and several jaw pieces.

Three weeks of intensive exploration uncovered several hundred more pieces of bone, which when pieced together proved to be parts of a single individual. Much of the skull was missing, but over 40 percent of the skeleton was recovered. The bones were interpreted as belonging to an adult female three feet eight inches tall weighing perhaps sixty-five pounds. Lucy, as she came to be called (after the then-popular Beatles song) was classified by the scientists as *Australopithecus afarensis*, a near relative of the Taung child of South Africa. Dating by the radioactive potassium-argon method revealed that she lived three million years ago, indicating that, except for a few questionable fragments of teeth and jaw, found elsewhere, Lucy was the oldest hominid ever found. Of most fascination was the discovery that she walked upright, the erect bipedal stride being established by the flared shape of the pelvis.

Later discoveries at Hadar included one small area in which the assorted remains of some thirteen individuals were recovered. Were they a social group struck down by some natural catastrophe? Given this possibility, they were popularly called "The First Family."

But the fossils at Hadar were of two sizes—one group, diminutive, like Lucy, and the other much larger. Johanson's first reaction was to assume that the two groups indicated two branches to the human tree, as Richard Leakey's Lake Turkana explorations suggested. But another possibility existed, which if true gives important data about the sociology of early hominids. That possibility is that the two different sizes represent sexual dimorphism, the large disparity in size between males and females often seen in primates. If that was the case, the Hadar individuals would represent only one species, *Australopithecus afarensis*, and be the only ancestor of the human species.

The controversy over one species or two still goes on between Johanson, Tim White of the University of California at Berkeley, and their colleagues on the one side, and Mary and Richard Leakey and their coworkers on the other. Lewin sums it up as follows:

> The naming of new fossils is often controversial—this occasion was no exception. It set Johanson and White and their followers against Mary and Richard Leakey and their followers: one species at the Hadar against two species, a recent origin of *Homo* against an ancient origin. The decade of debate over the issue has been vigorous, to say the least. Today, a straw vote among anthropologists would undoubtedly produce a strong majority favoring the idea that only one species existed at the Hadar site: *Australopithecus afarensis*. In this case, Lucy was indeed the diminutive female of the species, and her consorts, standing almost five feet tall, would have been twice her bulk. The Leakeys, however, remain unconvinced.[14]

If Johanson and his coworkers are correct, then a reasonable conclusion is that the thirteen individuals found together at Hadar were probably not a "first family" in the modern sense, but were more primitive in their social structure. Other ambivalences derive from the Hadar data as well. Lucy and her fellows were unusual. From the neck up they were primitive and from the neck down they were quite modern. An ape's head on a human body is a fair approximation. A small brain (one-third that of present humans) a low forehead, a bony ridge over the eyes, a flat nose, no chin, and large canine teeth and massive molars were all apelike characteristics. The rest of the skeleton was humanlike.

One thing seemed clear; bipedality came long before the larger-brain characteristics of modern man. Perhaps as much as two million years separated the origin of the upright walk from the larger brain. This is an important conclusion, for it raises significant questions for the popular idea that the human brain has always been the driving force for human evolution.

The oldest fossils that have the characteristics of bipedality were found in 1981 in the Middle Awash Valley some forty-five miles south of Hadar.[15] Tim White and a Berkeley colleague found several fragments of a skull and the upper part of a femur (the thighbone) that were dated at four million years. But how do we know from such limited evidence that these fragments were hominid? The answer was provided by CAT-scan images of the femur, which was shown to be thick in the lower portion but thinner farther up. That is characteristic of bipeds, but is not found in apes. In addition there was a characteristic depression in the femur at the same place that in modern humans is the grooved attachment site for one of the hip muscles, the *obdurator externus*.

As for the four-million-year dating of the fossils, that was made possible by virtue of the proximity of an ash layer called the Cindery Tuff, a marker bed dated by another radiometric method, argon 40/ argon 39 analysis. The use of tuff analysis and also a method called biochronology are favorite dating methods that often complement each other. In Weaver's words:

> Some of the best known tuffs, or volcanic ash layers, have been borne by air and water for substantial distances. Some are found at Hadar as well as at the Omo site in southern Ethiopia and around adjacent Lake Turkana in northern Kenya. The same chemical signature identifies a tuff in each place. Once the layer has been identified and dated at one location, the date is immediately useful in every other place the tuff appears.

> An indirect method of dating called biochronology depends on the assemblages of animal fossils found in particular strata. Tim White describes the Middle Awash, for example, as being "littered with fossils, from the jaw of a shrew to fossilized crocodile eggs." Among sedimentary layers there he and his colleagues have found an almost continuous fossil record, covering six million years, of extinct pigs, horses, baboons, hippos, and elephants. Since the Awash strata can be dated radiometrically, the evolving species of these animals can also be fixed in time. Thus a well-dated species of an extinct pig, for example, can give a rough idea of the age of a stratum for which geologic dating may be difficult or impossible.[16]

It was another deposition of tuff that provided one of the most dramatic discoveries in African anthropological history.[17] Mary Leakey had left her beloved Olduvai Gorge for another site called Laetoli, twenty miles to the south, because a single hominid tooth that had been found there by one of her associates was dated at 2.4 million years, older than anything at Olduvai. Laetoli is situated at the southern edge of the great Serengeti Plain, site of some of the world's most spectacular game migrations. Due east, some twenty-seven miles, is the vast crater of an extinct volcano called Ngorongoro. Within its ten-mile diameter are found thousands of plains animals and an alkaline lake that attracts a vast multitude of flamingos. To the east and north are other volcanic cones, each with its romantic Masai name: Lemagrut, Oldeani, Olmoti, Sadiman, Embagi. Further to the north is Oldongo Lengai, which means the Mountain of God in Masai. It is still active, periodically spewing clouds of steam and ash above the plain.

Unlike Olduvai, Laetoli is flat, a part of the windswept savanna, dotted by occasional acacia trees and covered with tough grasses and low bushes. It is the site of numerous animal trails, just as it must have been some 3.5 million years ago. The animals were somewhat different then; saber-toothed cats, ancient elephants with down-turning tusks, a pygmy giraffe and a horse-like animal with claws instead of hooves. But the volcanic activity was quite similar to that of the present day. Sadiman was the active volcano then, spewing out an ash mixture that had a component called carbonatite, just as present-day Oldongo Lengai. Carbonatite has the unusual property that when slightly wetted it dries into a cement-hard layer. It was this property that was crucial for the great discovery of Laetoli.

It was the end of the day, and two of Mary Leakey's coworkers, on the way back to camp, were amusing themselves by throwing pieces of dried elephant dung at each other. British anthropologist Andrew Hill ducked at one point and lost his footing. At the end of his fall, his eyes inches from the ground, he saw a set of petrified animal tracks, their blurred shapes amplified by the setting sun. Great excitement was followed by two seasons of excavation of the area that revealed a series of hominid footprints that were dated at 3.6 million years. The tracks were of three individuals and were very similar to the tracks of modern humans. In Mary Leakey's words: "The individual who made them must have been in the direct line of man's ancestry....Those prints demonstrate once and for all that man's earliest ancestors walked fully upright with a bipedal, free-standing gait."[18]

How did these tracks come to be? Mary Leakey suggests a probable scenario. It was the end of the dry season, with most of the grass grazed level and occasional, light showers signaling the coming of the heavy rains. From time to time Sadiman belched out its very special ash, which settled layer upon layer, over the parched Laetoli landscape. Apparently the eruptions were not fierce or intimidating, since the animals of the community went about their usual activities, leaving their footprints, twigs, bird's eggs, and dung to be covered by each new blanket of ash. Then a rain shower moistened the ash, and the carbonatite began its slow hardening, setting the ash and its animal record into a rock-hard layer. More ash fell, more animals passed by, and more rain fell. By the end of two weeks, a six-inch depth of ash had accumulated, layered like the leaves of a book, to preserve forever these events of 3.6 million years ago.

The three hominids who crossed this terrain at some point during those two weeks walked from south to north for at least seventy-five feet. At that point their tracks end in an erosion gully. Two of the tracks run side by side, one set of footprints larger than the other. The tracks are close enough that if the two individuals were walking together, then one must have walked slightly ahead of the other, or else they would have jostled each other off balance. The third hominid was the smallest, and left its prints superimposed on those of the larger of the pair, as though it was playing follow-the-leader. It was estimated that the larger individual may have been five feet tall and the smaller a little over three feet in height. The size of the very small individual could not be ascertained because of the superimposition of its footprints on those of the large individual. Mary Leakey's conclusion was that the small individual was a juvenile, the largest of the pair a male and the smaller a female. The tracks also reveal that at one point the female stopped, turned to the left slightly and then continued on. For Mary Leaky this event carried special significance. She says: "You need not be an expert to discern this. This motion—the pause, the glance to the left—seems so intensely human. Three million six hundred thousand years ago, a remote ancestor—just as you or I—experienced a moment of doubt."[19] For Mary Leakey, the Laetoli prints marked the long path toward *Homo sapiens* with an early touch of humanity and even the imprint of the nuclear family—mother, father, and infant.

The most recent chapter on fossil discovery begins with the appearance of yet another species of hominid, *Homo erectus*, which lived about 1.6 million years ago. It was apparently a contemporary of the australopithecines like *A. bosei* and also of *Homo habilis*, both of which left extensive remains at Lake Turkana in Kenya. Richard Leakey and his coworkers had already concluded, along with most other paleoanthropologists, that the human family tree was branched, a two-pronged fork with one tine, represented by *Australopithecus africanus* and *Homo habilis*, leading to modern humans and the other, represented by the heavy-jawed australopithecines, *A. boisei* and *A. robustus*, leading to extinction.

In the summer of 1975 Richard Leakey's team discovered a well-preserved cranium of a large-brained individual with fine facial features and small cheek teeth. It was dated at 1.6 million years and seemed considerably more advanced than even *Homo habilis*. *Homo erectus*, as it was called, had been hinted at in earlier discoveries there, but the most complete skeleton, of an adult female, was of disease-distorted bones that made firm conclusions about size and structure difficult.

By the summer of 1984, the explorations in Kenya had shifted to the western shore of Lake Turkana, and it was there that Kamoya Kimeu, Richard Leakey's partner for two decades, discovered what later proved to be the almost complete skeleton of a *Homo erectus* boy of about twelve years of age.[20] In size and proportion this individual, with the exception of his low forehead and beatle brow, would have passed for a modern twelve-year-old. His height, five feet four inches, was surprisingly large. The amazing conclusion: we may have reached our present stature 1.5 million years ago! Furthermore, future discoveries of *Homo erectus* have shown that the sexual dimorphism that was found with Lucy and her peers and continued with *Homo habilus* is greatly diminished. Males and females were much more nearly the same size in *Homo erectus*.

Other major distinctions come with *Homo erectus* as well. The capacity of early hominids to make stone tools dates from about 2.5 million years ago, but only with the advent of *Homo erectus* do tools begin to show a level of design and complexity, and only then is there use of fire and the signs of a hunter-gatherer society. Only with *Homo erectus* do we find individuals and groups moving between camps. And only *Homo erectus* migrated out of Africa! The four species of australopithecus and *Homo habilus* apparently are found only in Africa. *Homo erectus*, equipped with a larger brain and specialized stone tools, moved into North Africa, Southeast Asia, China, and probably also southern Europe. He seems to disappear from the fossil record about three hundred thousand years ago.

C. THE NEANDERTALS

According to Roger Lewin, one of the hottest topics in anthropology today concerns the place of the Neandertals in man's evolutionary history.[21] The Neandertals, whose average brain size was greater than present humans, can be traced back some two hundred thousand years. Their name comes from the German valley where their fossil remains were first unearthed in 1814. At first, these creatures were much maligned as nasty, brutish—even grotesque—for their short, stocky build, presumably stooped posture, large face, and heavy brow. It was later revealed that the early impressions were erroneous, at least in part because of symptoms of arthritis in the most studied and interpreted of the early Neandertal fossils. Gradually, too, it became apparent that these individuals were human in a way unlike anything seen earlier. For the first time in history, evidence revealed a race of hominids that performed ritual burials, a uniquely human activity. Individuals and whole families were buried with tools and flints and apparently food as well, as though they were being provisioned for an afterlife. One child's burial was marked by a stone slab smeared with red ocher, which often carries a ritual connotation. At about the extreme range of the Neandertals, which covered all of Europe and reached as far east as present-day Uzbekistan, at a cave site called Teshik Tash, a young child was buried with a headdress of six pairs of ibex bones. But the most fascinating of the ritual burials was uncovered in one of the most recent Neandertal sites, sixty thousand years old, the magnificent cave site of Shanidar in the Zagros Mountains of modern Iraq. Here, French investigators found traces of woody horsetail and pollen from a number of flowering plants—cornflower, yarrow, hollyhock, St. Barnaby's thistle, ragwort, and grape hyacinth. It has been suggested that the buried man may have been a medicine man or shaman. His burial must certainly have been a colorful and aromatic one![22]

Loren Eiseley, in his description of another famous Neandertal burial site, a French cave near La Chapelle-aux-Saints, catches the deeper meaning with these words:

> Massive flint-hardened hands had shaped a sepulcher and placed flat stones to guard the dead man's head. A haunch of meat had been left to aid the dead man's journey. Worked flints, a little treasure of the human dawn, had been poured lovingly into the grave. And down the untold centuries the message had come without words: "We too were human, we too suffered, we too believed that the grave is not the end. We too, whose faces affright you now knew human agony and human love."

> It is important to consider that across fifty thousand years nothing has changed or altered in that act. It is the human gesture by which we know a man, though he looks out upon us under a brow reminiscent of the ape.[23]

The Neandertals have been called the People of the Ice Age since their history covers much of the past two Ice Ages. They are believed to have fully differentiated as a unique species only by seventy thousand years ago, at the beginning of the last Ice Age. The previous Ice Age had ended one hundred thirty thousand years ago, and the warmer interglacial period from one hundred thirty thousand to seventy thousand years ago, might then have been the period of their maximum development. Ten thousand years later, as the ice sheet crept southwards again, they had reached their maximum migration to the east. The later history of the Neandertals, from seventy thousand years ago until their extinction thirty-five thousand years ago, was thus perhaps a history of unseccessful adaptation to severe cold and an overdependence upon reindeer, woolly rhinos, and mammoth for food and clothing.

But the disappearance of the Neandertals remains a mystery, especially since they had proved so innovative in the early part of their history. For these advanced hominids were innovative toolmakers who quickly brought the relatively crude and simple toolmaking of *Homo erectus* to a new level of sophistication. The method that they developed involved striking flakes of stone from a prepared disk-shaped core, and then trimming the edges of the resulting flake to make a stone tool. A single large rock, once it was trimmed into a disk-shaped core, could be the source of hundreds of flakes, the core being rotated slightly after each flake was chipped away, until the core had been converted almost completely to flakes. The flakes could then be trimmed and shaped to provide over sixty different tools—knives, scrapers, and gouges. Curiously, the Neandertals did not appear to make stone spear points. This technology has been called the Mousterian, after the French site where it was first discovered in 1860. Lewin remarks on its uniqueness: "The scope of the Mousterian technology was so much greater than its predecessors, and its duration so much shorter, that the pace of change in human history was comparatively breathtaking."[24] However, once the Mousterian technology had been introduced, there were no further changes for another fifty thousand years, until the Neandertal period ended and the modern human era began.

The archaeological context of the Neandertals lies in a critical transition stage in human history, between the primitive *Homo erectus* and the modern *Homo sapiens*. Neandertals lived in a period beginning sometime before two hundred thousand years ago and ending thirty-two thousand years ago. Their disappearance appears to have begun about forty-five thousand years ago in the Near East, and to have swept from east to west across Europe like a wave through time. What factors led to this rapid disappearance remains baffling. Its coincidence with a second migration out of Africa into Europe and Asia, this time by modern humans, suggests that replacement of Neandertals occurred during this period. Another possibility is that Neandertals simply interbred with the more modern *Homo sapiens*, and so disappeared as a distinct species.

Actually, the Neandertals were not the only hominid species involved in the transition period. Recall that the earlier hominid *Homo erectus* had moved out of Africa into the rest of the Old World some one million years ago, and disappeared from the fossil record in all areas some three hundred thousand years ago. Christopher Stringer, anthropologist at the Natural History Museum in London, tells us that at this point one begins to see fossils with a mosaic of ancient and modern features in various parts of the world including Britain, Germany, the Near East, and Africa. Archaic *sapiens* as these were called, were also found to exist some one hundred thousand years ago in Java and northeast China.[25,26] The question that arises is "Were these the precursors of modern humans?"

D. The Possibility of an African Origin of Modern Humans

Until the last decade or so, paleontologists had indeed assumed that modern humans arose from the various archaic forms found in different parts of the world. In this approach, the Neandertals would be the precursor of modern *Homo sapiens* in Europe and the Near East. This period has been called "The Neandertal phase," and places great emphasis upon culture as the driving force for human evolution, providing a new kind of selection based upon social and technical skills. Harvard anthropologist William Howells calls this descent through various archaic forms worldwide the "Candelabra theory," to emphasize the essential branching near the base of the human evolutionary tree. The origin of modern humans would involve *Homo erectus* as the source but with different paths in different parts of the world. The expectation would be that modern humans would appear almost simultaneously in widely different parts of the world. Racial differences among the world's populations would then be deeply rooted. This theory is strongly supported by many anthropologists, including Milford Wolpoff of the University of Michigan.

The second interpretation, which leans heavily on some very recent anthropological data and the new genetic data, proposes a single geographical origin for *Homo sapiens*, in Africa. Populations of this species would then have migrated out of Africa into the rest of the world, replacing existing primitive human populations, like the Neandertals, which they encountered. In this model, since all modern humans radiate from the common center, racial differences would be quite recent and therefore shallow. Howells calls this interpretation the "Noah's Ark Hypothesis."

It is also possible that some combination of the "Candelabra" and "Noah's Ark" interpretations could be the correct one, with perhaps a single African origin for modern humans but some intermixing of the gene pool of these new individuals with existing hominids. Considerable current evidence favors the Noah's Ark or out-of-Africa interpretation, especially the quite recent genetic evidence from studies of mitochondrial DNA (mt

DNA). Recall that it was the data of molecular geneticists Wilson and Sarich, based upon a kind of molecular clock, that led to the idea that apes and humans were closely related. That kind of work, done originally by comparison of blood proteins, has subsequently been carried out with DNA, and in particular with a certain kind of DNA found only in mitochondria, the cell organelles that provide the bulk of cellular energy in most organisms. Mitochondrial DNA has two distinguishing characteristics. One is that it is distinct from the DNA of the nucleus and the second is that its mode of inheritance is maternal. Whereas nuclear genes are inherited from both parents and shuffled in sexual reproduction, mitochondrial genes are contributed only by the female sex cells, so are handed down from generation to generation by the mother only. Additionally, mitochondrial genes are much more frequently mutated, a factor that makes mt DNA much more useful as a molecular clock, a device for assigning a date to every branching point on the genealogical tree.[27]

The initial work with human mt DNA has been carried out by Allan Wilson and coworkers at Berkeley. What they have done is to compare mt DNA from about 150 women from five geographical populations throughout the world—Asia, Africa, Europe, Australia, and New Guinea. When the DNA sequences were compared, the most striking thing was that there was little difference between the various groups, which implies that they separated from each other only recently. Another thing that was observed was that the DNAs fell into two main groups—one that represented only sub-Saharan Africans, and the other that represented individuals from all groups. And it was also evident that the sub-Saharan African group was the longest established of all. That is, the greatest sequence divergence—the largest number of mutational differences—was found when comparing the African group's mt DNA with a reference DNA. The principle here is that the most ancient human DNA, that from which all the others were derived, would be that with the greatest number of sequence differences. Thus, the mt DNAs from the sub-Saharan Africans were assumed to be derived from a common ancestor of all modern humans. This so-called mitochondrial Eve was from South or East Africa and was probably derived from an ancestor of the present-day Khoisan people of South Africa, perhaps one hundred thousand years ago. In other words, the mt DNA samples of the sub-Saharan group of six individuals contain the most divergent sequences—the most divergent human branches or lineages—and all live in a single population of Kung Bushmen in the Xangua Valley in northwest Botswana. It is most likely that these Bushmen are descended from a series of wandering bands that had separated from an original small population elsewhere, and it is possible that *all of us* are derived from the same small population!

Stringer points out that the mt DNA methodology upon which this conclusion is based has to meet several critical criteria. One is that, as we have said, genetic similarities must be directly proportional to the recency of their divergence from a common ancestor. It is also required that the DNA under study mutates at a constant rate and that mutations neither be culled or favored by selective processes. Culling would tend to conserve a given gene in its original unmutated form, and so give an erroneously young age for the common ancestor. Selection for particular mutations would accelerate change, making divergence seem more ancient. These last criteria appear to be met by certain portions of mt DNA for which no physiological function is known. Since mutations in these components do not affect the phenotype, they appear to be unaffected by selection processes. It is this fraction of mt DNA that has been analyzed.

The one major obstacle remaining for the geneticist is to establish that very little mixing occurred in the ancestral population as it migrated out of Africa, since introduction of genes from the more ancient species discussed earlier would throw off the molecular clock, making "Eve" seem more recent by adding back unmutated genes to her progeny. Such an effect could position the ancestor at more than twice the present one-hundred-thousand- to two-hundred-thousand-year-old estimate, and make the precursor more likely *Homo erectus*. However, some recent fossil evidence together with the analyses of population geneticists, tend to support the recent origin of modern humans in Africa.

The fossil evidence concerns the 1987–88 dating by thermoluminescence and electron-spin resonance techniques of modern-looking fossils from a cave called Jebel Oafzeh in Israel at one hundred thousand years of age, considerably older than Neandertal fossils from neighboring caves that were dated by the same techniques at sixty thousand years. Previously these cave populations had been interpreted in a manner to suggest that modern humans came after Neandertals and so were descended from them. The new dating indicates that modern humans and Neandertals may have existed side by side and that they apparently maintained their distinctiveness for thousands of years.[28,29]

The only other early modern human fossils are found in southern Africa, and are also dated, though less accurately, at one hundred thousand years of age. The best data seems to be from the Klasies River Mouth Cave, 270 miles east of Cape Town, where University of Chicago anthropologist Richard Klein has found humanlike upper and lower jaws, cranial fragments, isolated teeth, and limb bones. These anatomically modern fossils date from between one hundred fifteen thousand years and eighty thousand years ago.[30] Stringer suggests that these recent findings place the source of modern humans in Africa and the source of Neandertals in Europe, and warrant a separate, nonhuman designation for Neandertals *(Homo neandertalensis).*[31] He is quick to point out that this is a minority opinion at present, and that the progenitors of the modern humans in Africa have yet to be identified. But the current data seems to suggest a surprisingly recent origin of modern humans from Africa, perhaps from the northern reaches of the Rift Valley, geographically between the early moderns of South Africa and those of the Israeli caves.

One final point that could favor a very recent single origin of modern humans comes from an analysis of the mt-DNA data from the standpoint of the shape of the genealogical tree. Population geneticists observe that the separation of a single population into several distant populations will slow or stop the loss of previously existing sequences (those that are held in common) and accelerate the loss of new sequences (those that are locally unique) that appear within the new, smaller populations. The net result of the sudden expansion of the ranges of a species will cause a sudden increase in the number of branch points retained—a bulge in the genealogical tree. This is what is seen in the human mt-DNA analysis, but not in the mt-DNA data from the chimpanzee. Evolutionary biologist David Wilcox of Eastern College, who has pointed this out, concludes:

> Unlike the chimpanzee lineage, which has uniform branching back to its root, the human lineage has a very large bulge at a little less than half the distance back to its root. Chimpanzees have stayed in the African forests. Modern humans exploded across the map of the world around 40,000 years ago. If the bulge is that dispersal, the human common root is only about 85,000 to 105,000 years ago.[32]

E. The Remarkable Pace of Human Evolution

Once modern humans became established there was a veritable explosion of innovation. Painting, engraving, and tool manufacture changed so quickly that archaeologists divide the periods from thirty-five thousand years ago to ten thousand years ago into six separate cultural periods, each with its own style of technology and innovations. David Wilcox points out that by contrast the Neandertal populations displayed cultural stasis like *Homo erectus.* The Mousterian tool culture that they developed appeared around one hundred thousand years ago and remained basically uniform across Europe for sixty-five thousand years. The modern humans that apparently replaced the Neandertals were, in less than half their tenure, walking on the moon![33]

Surprisingly, the beginning of this period was about the midpoint of the last glaciation, when much of northern Europe lay buried beneath a vast ice sheet, in some places a mile thick. Sea levels were three hundred feet below present levels, and there were land bridges connecting North America with Asia, and Britain with continental Europe. Southern Europe was generally a grassland much like the African plains of today. When frequent temperature fluctuations brought some respite from the cold, woodland developed and some forest creatures appeared. But a few hundred years later, the ice returned again and the grasslands one again became prominent. The people of Ice Age Europe lived through unusual, changing times.

What were these modern humans like? Most emphatically, they were artistic. Perhaps this is a reflection of their forced confinement in caves during periods of bitter cold, but the contemporary Neandertals apparently display no such art in their cave dwelling. And what art these moderns produced! The seventeen-thousand-year-old Lascaux Cave, the most spectacular of the caves of Ice Age Europe, is filled with vivid images of animal activity. Roger Lewin captures some of the drama at the beginning of a tour of Lascaux with one of the cave's discoverers, Jacques Marsal as guide, as follows:

> Guided by a small handrail and the thin beam of Marsal's flashlight, you slowly edge some dozen yards along a crude pathway. Marsal tells you to stop and then moves away. His moment of drama has come. No one speaks. You wait nervously, your eyes straining to penetrate the cavernous darkness of the cave. Suddenly, the deep chamber floods with light, and you find yourself in the midst of chaotic visual activity.
>
> To your left, a small herd of horses gallops away from you, the manes flowing, apparently fleeing from a strange horned creature at their rear. A massive bull aurochs—forerunner of modern domestic cattle—runs with them. Two small stags confront them head-on, then three more bulls surge around the curved end of the chamber at a terrifying clip. The last bull measures twenty feet from horned head to muscular rump. Smaller bulls, horses, bison, and deer dodge and leap among the racing herds. The more you look, the more you see. Animals materialize everywhere.
>
> This is Lascaux, the most spectacular of all painted caves of Ice Age Europe. Here, encapsulated in sweeping lines and polychromatic images, are clues to a way of life of people who lived some seventeen thousand years ago. The power and depth of the images speak directly to us, and we instantly recognize something germane to ourselves—here indeed is a cogent expression of the Age of Mankind.
>
> Jacques Marsal's trick of taking visitors to the center of this first chamber of Lascaux—the Hall of Bulls—under cover of darkness and then throwing the light switch, never fails to stir the emotions. How could it not?

Here you stand, deep underground, surrounded by a scene so imbued with life that you can almost hear the thunder of hooves, smell the earthiness of the hides. Even the shadows cast by the billowing limestone roof add to the sense of surging energy. The myriad images are sharpened by the thin layer of white crystalline calcite that clings to much of the cave's rock face, a sparkling canvas for its ancient artists.[34]

The Hall of Bulls is the largest—fifty-five feet long by twenty-two feet wide by nineteen feet high—but by no means the only spectacle at Lascaux. Another room, immediately adjacent to the hall, is called the Axial Gallery. It is more confined, and greets the visitor with a single large red cow with a black neck and head on one wall, and on the opposite wall a stag lifting its head to roar. Beneath the stag a line of seventeen dots ends in a rectangle, one of the many mysterious geometrical signs in the cave. Further along are a pair of facing ibex, then more cows, several yellow horses, and more signs. Looking back toward the Hall of Bulls, you see images that appear to flow from one wall, across the ceiling, and down the opposite wall. Every space was used. Beyond, the Axial Gallery opens out to reveal a giant aurochs charging toward you, then various smaller figures, and finally a large horse. At the end stands a calcite-encrusted pillar, site of one of the most extraordinary images of Lascaux. Winding around the pillar is the image of a horse, lying on its back, legs flailing the air, mouth wide open. Only part of the picture is visible from any one side; the viewer must move around the entire pillar to see the entire upside-down horse. This work of art, and many others at Lascaux, must have demanded great skill and imagination, given the poor lighting and cramped space available to the artist. Others can be seen in another long passageway from the Hall of Bulls, where the walls are of softer rock. There are not only a profusion of paintings but also engravings made in the rock walls, some using the natural shapes of the rock to provide a special lifelike aspect.

The last room of Lascaux is 180 feet from the Hall of Bulls, deep in the earth. It is called the Chamber of the Felines, and features an assemblage of six lions in various characteristic poses. Curiously, several are tethered by lines hooked into their flanks, and there are crosses and other lines scattered among the animals. Lewin says that the scene suggests some kind of activity with the images, not just an image of activity.[35] The most popular interpretation of the cave art was presented by Abbé Henri Breuil, a French archaeologist, who suggested the idea of "hunting magic": that the images were painted to increase the chances for a successful hunt. Indeed, even among modern hunter-gatherer societies, there is a strong identification with nature, and the kill is almost as much the hunter's death as the animal's death. But the many cryptic symbols suggest even deeper meanings.

What were these people of the caves and the grasslands really like? Clearly, they were radically different from anyone who had gone before in terms of artistry and ingenuity, symbolism and ritual. They were *Homo sapiens*. They may well have been from Africa, with their roots in that Khoisan tribe of perhaps one hundred thousand years ago. If so, they must have come to Europe and Asia shortly after their origin, for we find them in the Israeli caves seventy thousand years ago and in France, Britain, and southern Russia more that thirty thousand years ago. Their skin probably was black, and the archaic human populations—Neandertals and others—they encountered in Europe were probably white. Over time, Lewin tell us, *Homo sapiens* would have become paler, an evolutionary adaptation to the decrease in the sun's intensity that would then enhance their capacity to synthesize vitamin D.[36] Also over time they would replace Neandertals and other archaic humans, perhaps in something of the way that seventeenth- and eighteenth-century Europeans replaced the American Indians, though there is not conclusive evidence of interbreeding of the modern humans of seventy thousand years ago with their archaic counterparts. The picture that comes to mind, if replacement is the case, is one of epidemics and warfare and competition for dwindling resources in the Ice Age. But the level of trauma may not have been as great as one might expect. Anthropologist Ezra Zubrow at the State University of New York at Buffalo argues, "A small demographic advantage in the neighborhood of two percent mortality would have resulted in rapid extinction of the Neandertals. This time frame is approximately thirty generations, or one millennium."[37]

III. The Deeper Meaning of Human Evolution

A. THE DEEPENING BIOLOGICAL QUESTIONS

This is an exciting time for the study of the emergence of modern humans. As in other areas of science we have examined, questions multiply with each answer given. Fascinating questions need to be answered about the role of the brain and of language in the emergence of cultures based upon symbols and abstractions. Stringer[38] looks for a unified theory to bring fossil, archaeological, genetic, and linguistic evidence together to verify the African origin hypothesis further. What conditions were unique to Africa to bring about the evolution and migration of hominids as studied by the Leakeys and Johanson and their colleagues? And most intriguing of all, why a second origin there, but this time a quantum leap to modern humans, followed by a second rapid migration out of Africa!

And still to be explained adequately is the rapid disappearance of

Neandertals and other archaic humans. Many anthropologists are still skeptical of the Noah's Ark hypothesis. Milford Wolpoff is one who believes there are already sufficient examples of archaic humans in transition to modern humans in parts of the Old World to substantiate the Candelabra theory.[39] He has been studying the fossil remains of early modern Europeans that to him look less African and more Neandertal-like. Others have found a strange diversity of appearance of early moderns in Australia. The first inhabitants are presumed to have arrived from southeast Asia some fifty thousand years ago, but during the ensuing twenty-five thousand years there appear to have developed two branches of modern humans, one with the usual lightly built skull and a second with the heavy skull of more primitive hominids. Could the latter be descendants of Java man, or is something else going on?

The future should provide new methodologies for the study of human evolution. It may even be possible to study DNA extracted from human fossils and make comparisons with ancestral patterns now being constructed from the living. But an explanation for human uniqueness probably lies far beyond our future genetic knowledge. After all, we are only two percent different from the chimpanzee by that criterion. David Wilcox argues that we must turn to the idea of hierarchies.[40] Recall that we talked about hierarchies in connection with the increasing levels of complexity when moving from fundamental physical descriptions to biological and then ecological and sociological descriptions of living things. Each successive level of complexity builds on the lower ones, and confirms their validity, but at the same time brings in new levels of understanding that are not reducible to those lower levels.

In comparing humans to other primates we indeed have many similar biological characteristics. We have manipulative hands and highly mobile (brachiating) shoulders and large brains, but we also have a unique bipedal locomotion and subtle differences in the air passages and tongue, changes that provide for the complex shaping of sounds. The combination of the possibilities for speech along with a greatly enlarged brain provide for the development of abstract symbols (as evidenced in the cave art) and the highly complex social exchange we call language. Ecologically, humans are extremely diverse. No species on earth is so widespread and diversified in terms of habitat, resource utilization, and societal plasticity. We are the adaptive animal! If an extraterrestrial biologist were asked to explain the difference between ourselves and our ancient ancestor the chimpanzee, who still is confined to the African jungle, he would probably suggest that something quite extraordinary must have happened. In David Wilcox's words:

"Our Martian friend would probably conclude that the human species has indeed recently penetrated a radically new adaptive plane, one as great as the invention of photosynthesis or multicellular life. Perhaps he would conclude that a kingdom level "speciation" event has occurred, the first since the Cambrian."[41]

B. A Theological Perspective

Howell's use of Noah's Ark as a means to describe the out-of-Africa hypothesis is not inappropriate. The sudden appearance of modern humans with all their new capabilities does encourage a serious look at what the materialist has called the "Judeo-Christian Creation myth." The Bible begins the story of the creation of mankind with the words, "Let us make man in our image, in our likeness, and let them rule over the fish of the sea and the birds of the air, over the livestock, over all the earth, and over all the creatures that move along the ground. So God created man in his own image, in the image of God he created him; male and female he created them."[42]

Theists would not be surprised by a recent origin and rapid evolution of modern humans. It does indeed seem a quantum leap from the animal world to a creature with such enormous potentialities for creativity, ethical reasoning and altruism—a "kingdom level speciation." It might be argued that the other primates are not only anatomically and genetically like us but that they too have characteristics that we ordinarily associate with humanness. Certainly the chimpanzee is capable of tool use, can perform sign language, show empathy, and build long-term relationships. However, there is no evidence that they make their simple tools according to a pattern, as though they had a conceptual image of what they were making, nor that their use of sign language has any sense of grammatical arrangement—any syntax—which is the essence of language.[43] Behaviorally, chimps show no ethical sense or any particular evidence for feelings of guilt if, for example, they have killed a fellow chimp. World authority Jane Goodall refers to them as the "innocent killers."[44]

The exclusively human characteristics that appear crucial are reason, language, and responsibility, and it is very difficult to see these as the "elaborations of epiphenomena resulting from unguided material events" as Gould has suggested. However, it is interesting that he is impressed with the uniqueness of our origin, for he says, "We are an improbable and fragile entity, fortunately successful after precarious beginnings as a small population in Africa, not the predictable end result of a global tendency. We are a thing, an item of history, not an embodiment of general principles."[45]

But we have indeed seen that the world of objects—both animate and inanimate—displays just such a global tendency toward self-organization but that the agency transcends merely unguided material events. The interaction of chance and necessity, of unpredictable possibilities explored by the operation of the laws of nature, provides for a remarkable selection process. As Polkinghorne says, "The universe is full of the clatter of monkeys playing with typewriters, but once they hit on the first line of Hamlet it seems that they are marvelously constrained to continue to the end of at least some sort of play."[46]

The nature of what we are biologically still eludes us, and we shout for a deeper meaning that may never come by way of our very best and most sophisticated genetics and anthropology. As with the countless stars, we too are a universe of complexity, a deeper reality, perhaps to be seen finally in spiritual terms, as an image of the invisible God. We are reminded of T. S. Eliot's words from *Four Quartets;*

> With the drawing of this Love and the voice of this Calling
> We shall not cease from exploration
> And the end of all our exploring
> Will be to arrive where we started
> And know the place for the first time.
> Through the unknown, remembered gate
> When the last of earth left to discover
> Is that which was the beginning[47]

Summary

The past three chapters on self-organization have been concerned with mostly very recent findings in chemistry, biology, and paleontology that introduce the new, creative paradigm. The present chapter shifts the focus to anthropology, and looks at the surprising developments of the past few decades in our search for our own ancestors. It is seen that there is a continuity between humans and the other primates, but that there are also remarkable differences. In particular, the pace of evolution of the hominids, as seen in the African studies of the Leakeys and Johanson and their coworkers, quickens to a dash when what appears to be a new invasion of humans from Africa enters Asia Minor and moves from east to west across Europe. The sophisticated tool technology, the exquisite cave paintings, the complicated ritual burials, the evidence of compassionate care of the sick displayed by these people combine to suggest a quite sudden emergence of what could rightly be called the "spiritual." In what sense could such developments be the result of "blind chance"? Can such purposeful creatures have arisen by a process without plan or purpose?

Again we have seen evidence for a master plan and a Master Planner, albeit within the context of a creation given freedom to experiment—chance and necessity working together in a truly creative relationship.

Human evolution, just as with the evolution of all living things, is seen to be full of surprises and emergences and discontinuities. It is hardly the kind of process the evolution textbooks of just a few years ago proposed. The mechanisms become more and more obscure, the kind of lockstep relationships we used to expect in scientific explanations become more and more unlikely. The reality of our ancestry is seen to be more meaningful in a theological than in a biological context. We are a onetime happening, never to be repeated, just as Gould suggests, but not because history is the final arbiter. If indeed, scientific concepts fail in their effort to explain, we see a deeper more profound explanation. God is the ultimate—and perhaps the only—Reality!

8

The Search for Reality

Introduction

Perhaps it is time for a review of what we have been saying about what we really know in science and how the data of science point to a deeper Reality

I. Changing Reality

A. CHANGING REALITY IN SCIENCE

We began this book with a chapter about the new understanding of the character of science. Just a century ago science appeared to be tidying up our world, dispelling the illusions of gods and inexplicable miracles and finally providing us with an "objective" world. Yet now, despite the fact that we live at a time of enormous advances in our knowledge of our universe, there are few who would claim that objectivity is realizable in science, and fewer still who would exclude the possibility that an invisible hand is involved in this vast process. For our science in this century has brought us relativity and quantum theory, and with them have come some strange new understandings of our world; space and time are no longer separable, the passage of time is variable, dependent upon the velocity of the mover, matter and energy are interchangeable, and cause and effect have no meaning at the level of sub-atomic interactions. The credo of objectivity, together with its tight little mechanisms and clockwork images, is gone. Matter has lost its tangibility and quantum physics has shown our world to be more like a symphony of wave forms in dynamic flux than some sort of mechanical contrivance.

Anthropologist Loren Eiseley talks about the illusions of science in his book, *The Firmament of Time:*

> A scientist writing around the turn of the century remarked that all of the past generations of men have lived and died in a world of illusions. The unconscious irony in his observation consists in the fact that this man assumed the progress of science to have been so great that a clear vision of the world without illusion was, by his own time, possible. It is needless to add that he wrote before Einstein...at a time when Mendel was just about to be rediscovered, and before the advances in the study of radioactivity had made their impact—of both illumination and confusion—upon this century.
>
> Certainly science has moved forward. But when science progresses, it often opens vaster mysteries to our gaze. Moreover, science frequently discovers that it must abandon or modify what it once believed. Sometimes it ends by accepting what it has previously scorned. The simplistic idea that science marches undeviatingly down an ever-broadening highway can scarcely be sustained by the historian of ideas.[1]

Scientific progress is always attended by the correction of error, and sometimes by sharp shifts in direction and emphasis. And the nature of the correction is again only tentative, only partial truth. And the illusions could hardly be said to have been dispelled. In fact, in a very real sense, what we have started with as the tangible—matter, energy, space, and time now seems to bear some of the mystery of an illusion. Things are not what they seemed. In the words of science writer K. C. Cole:

> So much of science consists of things we can never see: light "waves" and charged "particles"; magnetic "fields" and gravitational "forces"; quantum "jumps" and electron "orbits." In fact, none of these phenomena is literally what we say it is. Light waves do not undulate through empty space in the same way that waves ripple over a still pond; a field is only a mathematical description of the strength and direction of a force; an atom does not literally jump from one quantum state to another, and electrons do not really travel around the atomic nucleus in orbits. The words we use are merely metaphors. "When it comes to atoms," wrote Niels Bohr, "language can be used only as in poetry. The poet, too is not nearly so concerned with describing facts as with creating images."[2]

Cole's reference to the words used as "merely metaphors" is perhaps unfortunate. Recall that Ernan McMullen, in support of a special place for the scientific enterprises, favorably compares a scientific theory or model with the poet's metaphor. He says it is the metaphor that can lead the mind in ways that literal language cannot, illuminating something not well understood, something puzzling or mysterious. There is much to be learned from the poet!

And, as if this was not enough of a challenge for the scientist who is still mourning objectivity, next come the profound insights of philosopher Michael Polanyi arguing that the scientist's commitment to the essential truth he is seeking actually serves as a valid and even essential component in approaching reality.[3] We all live by faith!

Of course, not everyone in science has been impressed by the limitations we have mentioned. Stephen Hawking's theory of quantum gravity, which seeks to unify the four forces of nature, is to him so all-inclusive that he claims for it physical reality. The glaring difficulty with his proposal is that it is built without almost any experimental verification. Recall, too, Freeman Dyson's reaction that he doubted that physical reality could be described by a finite set of equations. Indeed, the ideal that a physical theory could explain everything faces the limitations placed upon it by its foundational position in a hierarchy of systems. Only the most extreme reductionist would claim that physics explains everything, as if our knowledge of the physical structure of the DNA molecule fully defined its meaning as genetic information. Biology has much more to say, though what it says should be consistent with the more fundamental science of physics.

B. Changing Reality in Theology

One of the most exciting things about the current situation in science is that many scientists are beginning to ask theological questions. We have mentioned William James and Alistair Hardy, Michael Polanyi and Albert Einstein as forerunners. We have also been impressed with Werner Heisenberg's religious convictions and have been moved by Loren Eiseley's deep sense of worship. Who can tell how powerful and fruitful will be the science of the future when men and women of science return in humility to that first great quest, to think God's thoughts after him?

But theology has changed as well, being affected by some of the same forces that have impacted science, with a resulting reassessment of the nature of theological doctrine and the meaning of theological language and metaphor. Theology too is in a new state of exploration of reality. One significant difference between science and theology persists. In the hierarchy of systems, theology seems to have a place above the sciences, because of its highly integrative approach. From our standpoint, bringing God, man, and nature together is the ultimate integration!

C. A New Integration: Science and Theology

Bringing scientists and theologians together within this framework of exploration would be a source of tremendous opportunity for extending our understanding of ourselves and of the spiritual dimension. Science has proved a powerful tool for bringing us new concepts about our universe—of its origin and its structure—and about our biosphere and its myriad manifestations of life. The sheer size and intricacy of what we study in science invokes a sense of awe and a feeling of humility. We believe that this expression of humility is fundamental to the success of integration—scientists and theologians alike humbled by the awesome majesty of the Creator and his Creation, freed of their pride and self-centeredness, and open to the many theological challenges of the new science. We see the future open to the scientific exploration of spiritual subjects such as love, prayer, meditation, thanksgiving, giving, forgiving, and surrender to the divine will. It may be that we shall see the beginning of a new age of "experimental theology," which may reveal that there are spiritual laws, universal principles that operate in the spiritual domain, just as natural laws operate in the physical realm.

A theology based on humility could also bring about a new Renaissance in our religious traditions, where our theology may find fresh interpretations, building on the strengths of the past with new insights from the physical and human sciences. A humble attitude will encourage thinking that is open-minded and suggest caution in avoiding overinterpretation. It will encourage diversity rather than syncretism, just as our universe is characterized by constant change, ever-increasing variety, and progressive development.

II. Failure of the Search for Physical Reality

A. THE GOAL OF UNIFYING THE FORCES OF NATURE

As we mentioned earlier, not everyone in science has seen the importance of an integration of science and theology. Many still cling to the notion that science holds the complete answer to reality. After all, they would argue, some things in science are far more secure—the periodic table of the elements, the laws of thermodynamics, relativity, the genetic code, biological evolution—and we are gradually building a foundation of fact that will lead to a clear picture of reality. Indeed, Stephen Hawking feels that his theoretical approach to the unification of the forces of nature is the final statement, so ultimate that he claims it even eliminates the need for any theological answer.

In chapter 3 we mentioned that the philosopher Immanuel Kant had given a special place to the idea of the unity of nature as one of the "regulative ideas" that satisfy our need for order. It is this concept that draws physicists toward unification. And we have reviewed the efforts of physicists to bring in some order, some simplifying assumptions, as the number and complexity of subatomic particles and fields of force has grown. For what once had been a relatively simple picture of an atom, a central nucleus containing protons and neutrons orbited by external planetary electrons has become a seething mass of virtual particles in busy interchange, and the position of the electron in the atom can now be discussed only in terms of probabilities and standing waves.

One promising simplification has come with the very important new concepts, established over the past two decades, that have attempted to understand the fields of force in which various subatomic particles were involved. The theory of quantum electrodynamics has provided a mathematical description of the mechanism of electromagnetism as an interchange of photons between electrons and other charged particles. More recently, a similar situation has been postulated for the strong force that binds protons and neutrons together in the nucleus. Here, an interchange of heavy particles called pi-mesons, or simply pions, occurs. But the quantum electrodynamics theory is in considerable trouble, because certain critical computations lead to baffling infinities such as the infinite mass, charge, and energy of the electron.

The classification of quantum particles according to the forces they experienced has seemed a useful simplification. Yet, it has led to a new kind of complexity, since the heavy particles of the nucleus, the protons and neutrons, have now been shown to be made up of still-smaller constituents called quarks, which occur in eighteen different varieties and are sorted out three to a particle. These entities are related by another mathematical formulation called quantum chromodynamics, which also brings in a requirement for another set of force particles, analogous to the photons of quantum electrodynamics, which are called gluons. There are eight different gluons required by this formulation, and together with the eighteen different quarks, arrive at a total of twenty-six particles associated with the strong force in the nucleus. And we do not yet know if the quarks may also be made up of smaller subunits, or whether the particles of the weak force—electrons, neutrinos, and so on—may also be made up of quarks.

The picture is one of a deepening complexity and intricacy. Morris's suggestion of physical reality as a kind of cosmic onion, with level below level in an endless progression, seems very appropriate. Reality in a physical sense seems to recede from us, as though the things we see are only fleeting images of the unseen reality that lies behind.

1. Cosmology and Symmetry

A second promising approach to simplification has come as cosmologists and particle physicists have addressed the nature of the forces that were acting as time was moved back further and further in the direction of the moment of creation. It had been noted that all the physical laws were in fact evidence of symmetrical relationships in nature; in each case a measurable quantity remains invariant under some transformation because a force acts to compensate for changes in the system. When such so-called gauge symmetries were examined for the four known forces—the strong and weak nuclear forces, the electromagnetic force and gravity—it was found that two of the sources were related by a broken symmetry. The electromagnetic force and the weak nuclear force appeared to have been derived from a single more symmetrical parent. At very high energies, almost at the capacity of any particle accelerator to duplicate, it was demonstrated that the force particles predicted for such a parent force were indeed produced.

The concept that arose from this first step was that the present universe may have arisen by a process of symmetry breaking, with the four forces of nature all together in a perfectly symmetrical relationship at the moment of origin of the universe. The present universe would then have evolved by a series of symmetry breakings, of which the break that produced the electromagnetic and weak nuclear forces was the most recent and least energetic. The problem of further proof—the substantiation of so-called grand unified theories, that all four of the forces were one at the creation—has been addressed without success over the past two decades. The negative results from the very few experimental approaches to the problem have led many physicists to criticize the concept as too premature and too theoretical. Yet, its failure has not prevented physicist Stephen Hawking from claiming that the concept, in the particular refinement he calls quantum gravity, is the ultimate statement of physical reality. Again the mathematical formulation involves major complexities, of which the use of "imaginary time" is perhaps the most difficult conceptually. Ferris's perspective is to relegate real time to our universe and imaginary time to that time "prior to the moment of creation."

All these efforts toward unification seem to many physicists and cosmologists to be extremely premature. Recall Julian Schwinger's conclusion that the rush for a unified theory represents an overt expression of hubris. We know so little about the energies involved, and the way the universe works. We have been surprised again and again in the past by fundamentally new understandings of how nature works, and it would seem perilous to assume that symmetry breaking gives us anything even approaching a clear picture of reality. Certainly, the mathematical success of superstring theory, with its radically new view of the structure of subatomic particles but its requirement for additional undetected dimensions beyond the three of space and one of time should give us pause.

We are feeling our way to the understanding of an incredibly complicated universe.

B. SELF-ORGANIZATION AS A CLUE TO REALITY

1. *Evolution as a Directed Process*

While unification has remained an elusive goal in understanding the cosmos and its origin, a new paradigm, diversity, with self-organization as its driving force, has brought a powerful new perspective to the question of origins. We have seen that the evolutionary process has been operative not only in the origin of living things, ourselves included, but it has also been intimately involved in the origin of the present structure of the universe. The picture is an astounding one, a view of creativity unleashed across the whole spectrum of matter, from the vast reaches of the galaxies to the first spiritual awakenings of the Neanderthals and the African Bushman who were apparently our immediate forebears, and on to ourselves and whatever lies beyond. And that creativity has been expressed, where we know it best, in the evolution of living things. For the incredible events of evolution were punctuated we now know, with quite miraculous emergences and extinctions. The extraordinarily complex origin of life, the sudden early appearance of multicellular animals in great profusion in the Cambrian, and the proliferation of mammals following the sudden extinction of the dinosaurs 65 million years ago argue for a marvelous creativity and connectedness. The process seems to seethe with new innovations and a superb timing that dispels any notion of blind chance. And the end result? Matter has become mind, and now contemplates its origin and its reason for being! There are here strong hints of ultimate realities beyond the cosmos!

Science has heretofore been ruled by the Newtonian and thermodynamic paradigms, viewing the universe as either an unchanging and static machine, or as a process moving inexorably toward degeneration and decay. But the evolutionary process first described for living things by Charles Darwin and Alfred Russel Wallace has always seemed inconsistent with Newtonian stasis and thermodynamic decay. And subsequent developments in cosmological science have demonstrated that the increased complexity and diversity inherent in biological evolution have also been characteristic of the entire universe from its origin. Indeed, there appears to be a continuity of organization into novel and increasingly complex structures and relationships involving new cooperative and organizational processes throughout the spectrum of transition from stardust to thinking man. How did these changes come about? What processes could be involved?

The most likely candidate for this thrust toward diversity is a poorly studied category of earth's processes that the chemist usually defines as nonlinear, far-from-equilibrium, and irreversible reactions. They are less well understood because they are complex and irregular processes that are usually studied by approximation. The general approach is to model the processes under study to some regular system that is linear. The problem with this approach is that the basic characteristic of the system, spontaneous order, is overlooked. Furthermore, most processes would be oversimplified, since it turns out that the vast majority of the processes of nature are of this nonlinear type.

2. The Continuing Surprises and the Failure of Explanations for Self-Organization

a. A Revolution in Physics

Paul Davies has told us that the discovery of the self-ordering character of nonlinear processes and the new awareness of their very frequent occurrence in nature has brought physicists to feel that their subject is poised for a major revolution. On one side will be the unifiers, those who seek to reduce all phenomena to a single explanation, to seek the ultimate principles that operate at the lowest and simplest level of physics. For the unifiers, the ultimate goal is a "theory of everything." The other side is represented by the diversifiers, who see the universe as a holistic phenomenon, with the emphasis on organization and function as integrated wholes. The question is whether the propensity of matter to "self-organize" is explainable by the known laws of physics or whether a completely new set of principles is involved. We agree with the majority of diversifiers who feel that new principles come into play at each successive level of complexity, and that these principles are susceptible to scientific study but not reducible to simple physicochemical explanation.

b. The Extraordinary Creativity of Evolution

When we face the issue of what is known about the biochemical mechanisms for the origin of living systems, we have to confess, along with Dean Kenyon, that there are serious reasons for doubting that any straightforward naturalistic explanation will be forthcoming. Kenyon argues that the most recent studies of biogenesis are so artificially simplified as to be useless; potentially interfering cross-reactions as well as the presence of optical isomers in prebiotic systems have been ignored. And he expresses concern for the enormous gap between the most complex "protocell" model systems of the laboratory and the simplest living cells such as Mycoplasma.

Here again we are faced with a question of forces moving in the process of self-organization that seem to transcend the explanations of science.

Looking beyond the questions of life's origin to the processes of biological evolution, we are confronted by a spectacular display of innovative and adaptive organisms interacting with an often incredibly supportive environment. Indeed, the actors in this drama exhibit such creativity that Louise Young describes the process as "form set free to dance through time and space." Just thirty years ago biological evolution was assumed to follow the Darwinian view of gradual increase in complexity of organisms with time. A simple mechanism of natural selection among a series of chance mutations seemed plausible. But recent studies of the time course of appearance of new organisms reveals a startling series of discontinuities. Life appears almost before the earth has had sufficient time to cool, and variety and complexity of form appear without the expected simpler precursors. Primitive bacteria and unicellular photosynthetic organisms similar to the present blue-green algae appear as fossils dating to 3.5 billion years ago. The early production of oxygen by photosynthesis and the subsequent formation of an ozone layer to protect life from ultraviolet radiation were also crucial developments. Here is a picture of a remarkable interplay between earth and its first living inhabitants.

Then eukaryotic cells—those bearing specialized apparatus for inheritance (nucleus) and energy production (mitochondria) and sometimes motion (cilia)—appeared about 1.5 billion years ago. It was these more complex cells which provided the raw material for innovation and experimentation, for new relationships like colonial living and sexual reproduction. Some of the colony formers built the coral reefs, and some of the more modern examples are our termites and bees. The first multicellular organisms, the primitive algae, appeared about 700 million years ago. The union of separate cells carried the important possibility for specialization, division of labor into more efficient units, yet would allow for their independent mobilization for general needs in emergencies. Here is one of the first examples of the wholeness and interconnectedness that seem to characterize living systems.

At about this time the first animals came in a veritable explosion of variety, as Stephen Gould points out in his description of the soft-shelled aquatic animals whose fossils occur in profusion in the Burgess Shale of British Columbia. Recall that he concludes that most of the designs are not perpetuated, and strangely, some of what might be considered the best fitted are slated for extinction. From this vantage point, he argues, the entire process of biological evolution is irrational and certainly unrepeatable. If the tape were rerun, he suggests, we would not be in the story again. But the fact that we *are* in the story makes this just the kind of unique series of events for which self-organization must take on a far deeper meaning.

The first land animals appeared about 400 millions years ago, at which time the biosphere had been altered to provide oxygen at present levels and a protective ozone layer. The transition to the land involved plants in the intertidal zone, organisms with strong body parts, anchoring structures, and heavy cell walls to avoid dessication. Louise Young tells us that there is a certain mystery about this transition to the land. The doctrine of slow alteration by chance mutation and selection would argue for retention of easy environments for maximum survival. Yet the adaptation to land proved enormously successful despite the more stringent requirements of structure and nutrition. Although only 30 percent of the earth's surface is land, over 80 percent of all species are terrestrial, and these are the most complex organisms known. Life seems not to follow the path of least resistance.

The first land plants photosynthesized through the green porous stems and had root hairs that gripped the soil and brought water to the branches. They probably were the early developers of a symbiotic relationship with primitive nitrogen-fixing bacteria that supplied nitrogen in the form of metabolic ammonia in return for the plant's provision of photosynthesis and a secure location. Symbiosis remains one of the crucial innovations among living things.

The first land animals came ashore shortly after the first plants. They were spiderlike and air-breathing and eventually gave rise to what Louise Young says are thirty-two distinct body plans. These include everything from sponges and corals to earthworms and their relatives, to insects, spiders and the like, mollusks, echinoderms, and vertebrates. All of this enormous variety has come to us by the evolutionary path—tortuous, devious, full of pitfalls and dead ends, festooned with the successful and littered with the debris of the failures. Some failures were of immense proportions, and were often completely out of the hands of the participants. The comet that apparently struck the earth 65 million years ago left the dinosaurs with no choice—their habitat changed drastically and they all perished.

Yet the removal of the dinosaurs provided an open door for the warm-blooded mammals, including ourselves. And their removal also coincided with an explosive appearance of the angiosperms—the flowering plants. Within a few million years, a tick of the clock by evolutionary standards, the entire face of the planet changed. It is said that the appearance of these plants, bringing with them crucial high-energy food sources for the proliferating mammalian species, occurred so suddenly that Darwin referred to them as an "abominable mystery." Recall Eiseley's view of this sudden co-incidence of the high-energy-requiring mammals and the flowering plants, that it represents one of the supreme achievements in the evolution of life. One cannot view such marvelously coincident phenomena as flowers and warm-blooded creatures without realizing that all of nature exhibits a connectedness, an exquisite interlinkage. Flowers did indeed change the face of the planet. And we would probably not be here without them.

Joining flowering plants with mammalian evolution seems a master stroke. One can call such a coincidence only happenstance, but such events seem to be repeated throughout the evolutionary process, and to suggest strongly that something much deeper and more profound is going on. Someone has said that coincidence is God's way of remaining anonymous!

c. The Origin of Humankind

The final chapter in the evolution of life is the most profound of all— the origin of humankind. It contains the strongest evidence for purpose, since it brings with it most wondrous phenomena, human self-consciousness and the human spirit.

The beginnings of this miraculous emergence appear to go back some three million years, to the first hint of toolmakers in the rift valley of Africa. The first African discovery, made some six decades ago by Raymond Dart in a South African limestone quarry called the Taung Cave, was of a small skull that was suggested to be that of an upright-walking "manlike" ape dating back two million years. Dart's creature, called *Australopithecus africanus*, attracted anthropologists Louis and Mary Leakey to Africa, where they settled at Olduvai Gorge at the edge of the Serengeti plain in Tanzania. Their research spanned more than fifty years, and initially uncovered hominids and their tools that were closely related to Dart's "Taung Child," and then later fossils of the more delicately built and larger-brained *Homo habilus*, or Handy man, which was probably the first representative of our own genus.

Additional examples of early hominids were subsequently found at Lake Turkana in northern Kenya by Richard Leakey, son of Louis and Mary. In fact during the first ten years of the Lake Turkana explorations, the remains of over two hundred hominid individuals, including some twenty complete or almost complete skulls, had been discovered. Many of the fossils were classified australopithecines. Many others were more slightly built with more delicate features and larger brain size, and were given the designation *Homo habilis*. And there were some individuals that were enigmatic, and seemed to beg for some new classification. But the general impression that seemed to be emerging from the Lake Turkana fossils was that two million years ago there were two main branches to the human family tree;

Homo, which eventually led to modern humans, and *Australopithecus*, which eventually became extinct.

The oldest known hominid was discovered in 1974 by another anthropologist, Donald Johanson, who was exploring the Afar badlands of Ethiopia, at the northern end of the Rift Valley. He and his colleagues pieced together the fossil bones of a single individual, apparently an adult female three feet eight inches tall weighing perhaps sixty-five pounds. Lucy, as she came to be called, had the skull of an australopithecine and walked upright. Dating by the radioactive potassium-argon method revealed that she lived three million years ago. Subsequent finds by Johanson's group included large numbers of Lucy-like individuals that sorted into two size groups, a smaller size like Lucy and a larger group that were apparently males of the same species.

The most humanlike fossils were discovered by Richard Leakey in the following year at Lake Turkana, and were dated at 1.6 million years. They were called *Homo erectus*. Major distinctions appear between this species and the earlier hominids. For example, the capacity of early hominids to make stone tools dates from about 2.5 millions years ago, but only with the advent of *Homo erectus* do tools begin to show a level of design and complexity, and only then is there use of fire and the signs of a hunter-gatherer society. Only with *Homo erectus* do we find individuals and groups moving between camps. And only *Homo erectus* migrated out of Africa; the four species of australopithecines and *Homo habilus* apparently are found only in Africa. *Homo erectus*, equipped with a larger brain and specialized stone tools, moved into North Africa, Southeast Asia, China, and probably also Southern Europe. He seems to disappear from the fossils record about three hundred thousand years ago.

d. Neanderthals

The descendant of *Homo erectus*, in Europe was apparently the heavily built and larger-brained Neanderthal, at first maligned but later realized to be more humanlike than anything that had come before. Recall that these creatures performed ritual burial. Individuals and whole families were buried with tools and flints and apparently food as well, as though they were being provisioned for an afterlife. The disappearance of the Neanderthals remains something of a mystery, especially since they had proved so innovative in the early part of their history. These advanced hominids were innovative toolmakers who quickly brought the relatively crude and simple toolmaking of *Homo erectus* to a new level of sophistication. The Mousterian technology that they developed, striking flakes of stone from a prepared disk-shaped core and then trimming the edges of the resulting flake to make a stone tool, enabled them to make a whole new variety of stone tools. Surprisingly, once the Mousterian technology had been introduced, there were no further changes for another fifty thousand years, until the Neanderthal period ended and the modern human era began.

Recall from the last chapter that the archaeological context of the Neanderthal lies in a critical transition stage in human history, between the primitive *Homo erectus* and the modern *Homo sapiens*. Neanderthals lived in a period beginning sometime before two hundred thousand years ago and ending about thirty thousand years ago. Their disappearance appears to have begun about forty-five thousand years ago in the Near East, and to have swept from east to west across Europe like a wave through time. This rapid disappearance coincides with a second migration out of Africa into Europe and Asia, this time by modern humans, suggesting that replacement of Neanderthals occurred during this period. Another possibility is that Neanderthals simply interbred with the more modern *Homo sapiens* and so disappeared as a distinct species.

The Neanderthals were not the only hominid species involved in the transition period. Recall that the earlier hominid *Homo erectus* had moved out of Africa into the rest of the Old World some one million years ago, and disappeared from the fossil record in all areas some three hundred thousand years ago. Anthropologist Christopher Stringer noted that at this point one begins to see fossils with a mosaic of ancient and modern features in various parts of the world, including Britain, Germany, the Near East, and Africa. Archaic *sapiens*, as these were called, were also found to exist some one hundred thousand years ago in Java and Northeast China. The big question was "Were these the precursors of modern humans?"

e. Evidence for a Remarkable Origin of Modern Humans

Until the last decade or so, paleontologists had assumed that modern humans arose from the various archaic forms found in different parts of the world. In this approach, the Neanderthals would be the precursor of modern *Homo sapiens* in Europe and the Near East. William Howells calls this descent through various archaic forms worldwide the "Candelabra theory," to emphasize the essential branching near the base of the human evolutionary tree. The origin of modern humans would involve *Homo erectus* as the source but with different paths in different parts of the world.

The second interpretation, which leans heavily on some very recent anthropological data and very new genetic data, proposes a single geographical origin for *Homo sapiens* in Africa. Populations of this species would then have migrated out of Africa into the rest of the world, replacing existing primitive human populations like the Neanderthals. Howells calls this interpretation the "Noah's Ark hypothesis."

It is also possible that some combination of the "Candelabra" and "Noah's Ark" interpretations could be the correct one, with perhaps a single African origin for modern humans but some intermixing of the gene pool of these new individuals with existing hominids. Yet the weight of current evidence favors the Noah's Ark or out-of-Africa interpretation, especially the quite recent evidence from studies of mitochondrial DNA (mt DNA). Recall that mt DNA has a simplified form of inheritance, involving only maternal genes, and a rapid mutation rate, features that combine to make it useful as a molecular clock. In the pioneer work of Allan Wilson, mt DNA from women from five geographical populations were found to be quite similar, suggesting that the various populations separated only recently. A second thing that was observed was that the DNAs fell into two main groups—one that represented only sub-Saharan Africans, and the other that represented individuals from all groups. And it was also evident that the sub-Saharan African group was the longest established of all. That is, the greatest sequence divergence—the largest number of mutational differences—was found when comparing the African group's mt DNA with a reference DNA. Thus, the mt DNAs from the sub-Saharan African could have been derived from a common ancestor of all modern humans. This so-called "mitochondrial Eve" was probably from South or East Africa and was probably derived from an ancestor of the present-day Khoisan people of South Africa, perhaps less than one hundred thousand years ago. These Bushmen may have descended from a series of wandering bands that had separated from an original small population elsewhere, and it is possible that *all of us* are derived from the same small population. This astounding conclusion makes human evolution a rather colossal emergence!

We have reviewed the assumptions made in the DNA methodology; that genetic similarities are directly proportional to the recency of their divergence from a common ancestor, that the mutation rate is constant, and that no selection process intervenes either to retain or cull certain genes. Thus far these assumptions seem to be valid. It is also assumed that there was relatively little mixing of the ancestral population with other hominids as it migrated out of Africa, a process that would give an erroneous young date for a maternal ancestor. This, too, has received some verification.

The further validation of these assumptions would strongly support the recent origin of modern humans in Africa.

f. The Incredible Pace of Human Evolution

The question of the validity of a second African origin for *Homo sapiens* does not preclude our amazement at the remarkable pace of human evolution. Once modern humans became established there was a veritable explosion of innovation. Painting, engraving, and tool manufacture changed so quickly that archaeologists divide the period from thirty-five thousand years ago to ten thousand years ago into six separate cultural periods, each with its own style of technology and innovations. David Wilcox has pointed out that by contrast, the Neanderthal populations displayed cultural stasis like *Homo erectus*. As we have said, the Mousterian tool culture that they developed around one-hundred-thousand years ago remained basically uniform across Europe for sixty-five-thousand years. The modern humans that appear to have replaced the Neanderthals were, in less than half their tenure, walking on the moon!

What were these early modern humans like? Most emphatically, they were artistic. Perhaps this is a reflection of their forced confinement in caves during periods of bitter cold, but the contemporary Neanderthals did not draw in their cave dwellings. And what art these moderns produced! The seventeen-thousand-year-old Lascaux Cave, the most spectacular of the caves of Ice Age Europe, is filled with vivid images of animal activity that have a definite mystical ritual quality. And caves with drawings dot the map of Europe and the Mideast. Along with cave paintings we also find pieces of engraved bone, often with curious sets of markings that appear to have some mathematical significance, and a rapidly accelerating innovation in tool manufacture.

What were these people of the caves and the grasslands really like? Clearly, they were radically different from anyone who had gone before in terms of artistry and ingenuity, symbolism, and ritual. They were apparently from Africa, perhaps with their roots in that Khoisan tribe of one hundred thousand years ago. They must have come to Europe and Asia shortly after their origin, for we find them in the Israeli caves seventy thousand years ago and in France, Britain, and southern Russia more than thirty thousand years ago. In time they apparently replaced Neanderthals and other archaic humans. Curiously there is relatively little evidence of interbreeding.

We are not surprised by the recent origin and rapid evolution of modern humans. But from an evolutionary standpoint it does indeed seem a quantum leap from the animal world to a creature with such great potentialities for creativity, ethical reasoning, and altruism—a "kingdom-level speciation." It might be argued that the other primates are not only anatomically and genetically like us but that they too have characteristics that we ordinarily associate with humanness. Certainly the chimpanzee is capable of tool use, can perform sign language, shows empathy, and builds long-term relationships. However, as we have seen, there is no evidence that chimps make their simple tools according to a pattern, as though they had a conceptual image of what they were making, nor that their use of sign language has any sense of grammatical arrangement—any syntax—which is the essence of language. Behaviorally, chimps show no ethical sense or any particular evidence for feelings of guilt if, for example, they have killed a fellow chimp. This is why world authority Jane Goodall refers to them as the "innocent killers."

The exclusively human characteristics that appear crucial are reason, language, and responsibility, and it seems highly unlikely to us that these are the "elaborations or epiphenomena resulting from unguided material events" as paleontologist Stephen Gould has argued. It is interesting that he is impressed with the uniqueness of our origin—its unpredictability and singularity—yet, he seems eager to point out that no general principles underlie our coming to be! However, we feel it would be difficult to dispute the idea that there is some deeper explanation, some profound meaning behind the enormously creative process we have called self-organization. For this general principle, as we have seen, has been there in all its fruitfulness since the stars first began to shine. And it has moved with marvelous creativity within a structure of opportunity and cooperativity toward ever higher levels of complexity and sophistication to arrive at us! Where our scientific explanations fail, and we grope for new laws and new principles to account for the evolutionary process, we find it more and more appropriate to provide a theological explanation for this marvelous phenomenon, "form set free to dance!"

III. A Theological Perspective on Reality

A. GOD'S ACTION IN THE WORLD

One of the major themes of this book has been the dynamic and intimate involvement of the Creator in the processes of this world. In chapter 4 we referred to Donald MacKay's view of God as the Divine Artist who fashions a constantly changing panorama of unfolding events, actually "holding in being" the whole multipatterned drama of the universe. The emphasis in this analogy is on the sovereignty of God and his direct involvement in his Creation. And the consistency and regularity of the pattern are the proof of his faithfulness. God is thus the arbiter of the entire sweep of Creation, from the big bang, through the formation of star systems and supernovae from which heavy elements were made, to the origin and evolution of life on at least one planet in one solar system.

The difficulty with this view of God's role is that there is much that is apparently flawed about this process, and Louise Young is quick to say that this is hardly what one would expect for the unfolding work of an Almighty Creator. How could an omnipotent Creator design a world so full of happenstance and struggle, and with such embarrassments as species extinctions?

This question becomes even more urgent in the context of the origin of living systems that we discussed in chapter 5. Freeman Dyson's theoretical model of a primitive living system sheds some light on the difficulties that have been encountered in research on life's origin. Dyson's model allows for the calculation of the probability of a primeval molecular population jumping between two states that differ by the presence or absence of metabolic organization. In the rare case of the presence of metabolic organization, we have a living system. An ordered state exists in which the various catalytic cycles collaborate to generate energy and produce structure. Curiously it turns out that an essential requirement for the possibility of a statistical jump from disorder to this ordered state is the ability of the system to tolerate error. With an error rate of 20 to 30 percent, the majority of protein structures can still form correctly, and catalytic activity can thereby be preserved. Most important, this error-tolerant but nonreplicating model can embrace a hundredfold larger population of molecules, a population large enough and complex enough to make the transition from disorder to order statistically feasible.

So two conclusions arise from this work. One conclusion is that life needs to be complicated, since it is dependent upon necessarily complicated homeostatic mechanisms. Darwin had noticed this when he referred to the "tangled profusion" of life. Dyson combines this idea with error-tolerance and refers to the first cells as "error-tolerant tangles" of nonreplicating molecules. Noting that similar behavior is seen in ecology and in economic systems, Dyson proposes a "biological moral"—that nature is complicated and that something intrinsic in the error-tolerance of nature is fundamental to living systems.

Again we are confronted by the question of how a world of disorder and extinction and error can be ruled by a faithful and omnipotent Creator? Recall that physicist-theologian John Polkinghorne addresses this question in terms of a second view in which God's activity is more open and experimental. He proposes that two of God's salient characteristics, love and faithfulness, are actually more consistent with the world we see, a world of random events operating within a structure of natural law, a world or chance and necessity. God's love gives freedom to his creation for trial and error through the operation of chance while his faithfulness is expressed in the laws that act to select and retain useful innovations. Polkinghorne readily admits that this concession on God's part to give freedom to his Creation does open the way for disorder as well—earthquake, famine, epidemic, and the like—as consequences of genuine freedom. But that same freedom allows the Creation to seek out its full potentialities in a truly free creative interaction of its parts. And the result has been an unimaginably fruitful and dynamic process that has led, recalling Loren Eiseley's words, to "fiddling crickets, song sparrows, and wondering men."

B. MAYBE THE ONLY REALITY IS GOD

1. The Changing Picture in Science

We have mentioned previously that there has been heretofore a common misunderstanding in our scientific culture that a scientific understanding makes any other explanation superfluous. It is now clear that science owns no such exclusive position; that the best that we can do is to adopt a scientific realist position that accepts the theories and models of science as only approximations of the structures of reality. And the degree to which a given theory may provide an increasing sense of confidence that we are approaching reality is dependent upon how well that theory functions in prediction and control, in the design of new experiments and in escaping falsification!

Despite this realization on the part of most scientists of the limitations of scientific theorizing, we are amazed at the proposal of Stephen Hawking that his theory of quantum gravity is to be given the status of physical reality, as a kind of theory of everything. Freeman Dyson has reacted by pointing out that it is unlikely that the origin of the universe could be reduced to a simple equation because the laws of physics are probably inexhaustible, basing his argument on the famous Godel's theorem, which establishes the inexhaustible nature of mathematics. And perhaps most telling of all is John Wheeler's criticism that the theories that seek to unify the forces of nature are almost completely devoid of experimental support.

Of course, the idea that one discipline, physics, might give us a theory of everything is seriously questioned by what we have said about science as a hierarchy of disciplines. In the progression from physics to chemistry to biology to ecology, each successive science becomes enriched in empirical content, and new concepts emerge at each level that are entirely novel and not present in the preceding levels. Statements that are valid for lower levels are also true at the higher ones, but concepts that appear at a higher-level discipline have no definition at the lower level. The example we gave was the biological phenomenon of adaptation that has no definition in physics or chemistry. So science's quest for anything approaching reality must embrace the input from all disciplines.

But even within this larger integration, we are impressed that science appears to be facing a crisis of explanation. In chapter 4 we pointed out that there are two competing programs to explain origins. There is the program of the unifiers, seeking a theory of everything by going back to the beginning, and an equally vigorous program by the diversifiers, seeking an understanding of physical reality in terms of the organization and function of integrated wholes. The question for the diversifiers is "Can the propensity for matter and energy to self-organize be explained by the known laws of the physical and biological sciences?" Some diversifiers think not, and propose a picture of self-organization as a totally original process with its own laws and principles that are unique to a highly integrated, holistic phenomenon. Taken together with other challenges to explain reality—the quantum measurement problem and the complexity of the mind-brain relationship, for example—we seem to be long on speculation and short on explanation. Reality is deeper than we are!

2. The Changing Picture in Theology

If science's grip on reality seems to be loosening, so also is religion's. The view of reality that religion provides and theology interprets has undergone marked changes in attitude toward Scripture and the various religious traditions. Arthur Peacocke sees this as a healthy reassessment of the nature of theological reality, regarding the doctrines and symbols of theology as partial and limited but nevertheless essential ways of seeking to express the Reality of God. He points out that theology carries a special distinction because of its highly integrative character, bringing together God, man, and nature. The models and metaphors of theology are therefore of necessity more complex than those of the sciences, and its view of reality highly integrative and anthropomorphic. And just as with the sciences, the fact that theology is studied and articulated within a historical community or tradition makes its description of reality more susceptible to cultural and linguistic influence. In fact, it seems to us that the community exercises an even greater restraint in theology than in the sciences, and new ideas and concepts are less easily considered by the theologian than by the scientist. It is probably for this reason that the current interest in natural theology shown by scientists is not matched by theologians, despite the fact that these new concepts could provide enormous benefits to religious communities.

As an example of the opportunities, John Polkinghorne has been writing about the important contribution that current science can make to our notion of divine action. Recall that in chapter 4 we considered the new arrow of time, pointed in the direction of ever more developed and elaborate states of matter and energy. The mediators of this evolutionary process are complex and irregular nonlinear reactions that under far-from-equilibrium conditions can give rise to spontaneous order. Reactions of this kind display chaotic behavior, shifting back and forth between states of order and disorder as energy either becomes available or is dissipated.

John Polkinghorne points out in his recent book *Reason and Reality*[4] that chaos is not limited to highly complex reactions, but is even seen in simple equations such as those that describe population growth in biological systems. The relationship appears perfectly deterministic, yet the population at any time is found to be extremely sensitive to the choice of starting value of population size. As he says: "It is characteristic of chaotic systems generally that unless one knows the initial circumstances with *unlimited* accuracy, one can only project their behavior a small way into the future with any confidence. Beyond that they are intrinsically unpredictable."[5]

And he confesses his own surprise:

> The general picture resulting from these considerations is that of deterministic equations giving rise to random behavior; of order and disorder interlacing each other; of unlimited complexity being generated by simple specification; of precise equations having unpredictable consequences. That there are these possibilities is very surprising to those of us who were brought up on the study of those "tame," predictable mathematical systems on which we cut our mathematical teeth and which provided the standard teaching example for generations of students. The recognition of structured chaos has been hailed as a third revolution, worthy to be set alongside the Newtonian and quantum mechanical revolutions which preceded it.[6]

And as we argued earlier, here is a world in which novelty and order are intertwined. It is the kind of open-ended world in which a God who is both loving and faithful can take an active role. His action can be mediated both through the interaction of law and chance and through introduction of new form and direction at the infinity of starting points and branching points in nonlinear, chaotic processes.

All that we have said seems to shout for a God of marvelous creativity who mediates a world in dynamic flux, a world moving in the direction of ever more complex, more highly integrated form—form set free to dance.

As Louise Young has suggested, everything is in a state of transition.

Molecules, organisms, species are not fixed states of being, but rather stages of becoming. The current perspectives on reality of both science and theology seem to grasp dimly the edges of this grand paradigm of becoming. Perhaps in the end it is only God who expresses this ceaseless progression toward the highest integration and the greatest complexity. Perhaps in the end the only reality is God.

9

Where Do We Go from Here

I. Introduction

We know that the question of reality is dear to the scientist. Yet, from what we have considered in this book, there seems little likelihood that that question will be answered. The theologian is more relaxed about reality—he or she is dealing with God, and knows that such a transcendent theme defies definition.

What we have tried to show in this book is that neither scientist nor theologian, nor any other seeker for truth for that matter, will ever find reality as a final statement in their field, a "theory of everything." The nature of truth seems to be that it ever recedes from our grasp. Reality is deeper than we are!

What seems also to be the case is that the seeker after truth in one field cannot afford to ignore those in other fields. Truth has a wholeness that demands integration by the searcher The search for reality, though extremely difficult, is greatly enhanced by realizing the interconnectedness of knowledge.

This is not to imply that therefore there is no reality—that it is *only* an attempt at construction by our brains. For what is true *can* be validated, as Michael Polanyi has shown in his book *Personal Knowledge*.[1] Perceptions we may have aplenty, but our minds are so constructed that we may choose accurately among the alternatives. Indeed, this is one of the most staggering things about truth. It validates itself. Indeed, Albert Einstein spoke of the staggering fact of its comprehensibility.[2]

Polanyi added that there is a faculty that we require to arrive at truth in every field. That faculty is faith—a *commitment* to finding the truth—a feeling after the truth by way of "a passionate contribution in the personal act of knowing." The truth that we find there, the measure of reality that we achieve, comes to us less because of the excellence of our scholarship or the precision of our measurements—though these are often important ingredients—but primarily because of a special attitude, a faith that the truth is there to be understood, to be grasped by us.

And we believe the essential ingredient in achieving that attitude of openness is humility before the Creator God. We have reviewed the amazing process of evolution by which we appear to have come to be. This alone should be a humbling experience, as we realize the long and tortuous path we have traveled from such humble beginnings, and the brevity of our history on this planet—a mere tick of the clock on the evolutionary time scale. And we see no reason from a biological standpoint for our expectation of a long and supreme human history to follow. Even theologically it would be hubris to assume that God has no other plans for spiritual creatures beyond us—either here or elsewhere in the vast universe. Our human hope may lie in a God whose love and mercy exceed any human criterion. The biblical solution for mankind is resurrection to eternal life through faith in Jesus Christ. Other religions take us from this scene as well.

When we come to appreciate all these limitations—the extremely thin veneer that is our knowledge of the universe, our limited perspective with respect to the breadth of reality, and our own precarious place in the vast scheme of things, we might well expect a failure of nerve or a crisis of ego. But this is just the point where we ought to be, if we are to experience humility. For the pride and self-esteem that our society so prizes and encourages is the very root of our problem, because it ignores our proper relationship to the Creator God who is the Life giver and the Light giver.

II. Toward a Theology of Humility

In an earlier book we have talked about the Creator of the universe as the Light giver who seeks to reveal Himself in our universe through intricate design and purpose,[3] and we have talked in this book about God as the Life giver, whose love and faithfulness are revealed in human freedom and natural law—chance and necessity working together to create a world of infinite variety and beauty—form set free to dance. We have been struck with the remarkable contrast between ourselves—minute specks in one tiny star system in one of the smaller galaxies of the known universe—and the God who brought all this into being. From this vantage point we are impressed with the irony of statements by some small minority of scientists that their ideas of the universe might preclude the need for a Creator. It seems rather like Joseph Bayly's parable of the two computers having a learned discussion about whether man exists![4] And we are also impressed with how often religious leaders insist that their interpretation of the truth of God excludes any alternatives. By this means many who could begin the walk of faith are turned away. At its most flagrant, prideful pronouncements of religious dogma have provoked wars and strife and made mockery of the love of God.

Jesus quoted Isaiah thus: "But in vain they do worship me; teaching for doctrine the commandments of men."[5] Schisms in religions are caused by intolerance: and intolerance is a form of egotism. However, just tolerance of other religions is not what is sought in a theology of humility.

As one of us (John M. Templeton) has written previously:

> We should seek to benefit from the inspiring highlights of other denominations and religions, not just to tolerate them. We should try our very best to give the beauties of our religion to others, because sharing our most prized possessions is the highest form of "Love thy neighbor." Let us not water down the diverse religions into a know-nothing soup; but rather let us study enthusiastically the glorious highlights of each. An old Chinese precept is, "The good man does not grieve that other people do not recognize his merits. His only anxiety is lest he should fail to recognize theirs." It is a mistake for people of different religions to try to agree with each other. The result is not the best of each but rather the watered-down, least-common denominator. What is more fruitful is a spirit of humility in which we recognize that no one will ever comprehend all that God is. Therefore, let us permit and encourage each prophet to proclaim the best as it is revealed to him. There is no conflict unless the restrictive idea of exclusiveness enters in. We can hold our ideas of the Gospel with the utmost enthusiasm, while humbly admitting that we know ever so little of the whole and that there is plenty of room for those who think they have seen God in a different way. The evil arises only if one prophet forbids his audience to listen to any other prophet. The conceit and self-centeredness of such restriction—the false pride of saying that God *can* be only what we have learned Him to be—should be obvious....
>
> When the disciples of any cause, sacred or secular, stop seeking and claim they have the answer, the movement ossifies. It appears that God's creative method is movement, change, continuing search, ongoing inquiry. Those who seek are rewarded. Those who are sure they already have the answers gradually become obsolete. Perhaps "built-in" obsolescence is God's plan for keeping the world of ideas forever young, fresh, and invigorating. The self-confident proud grow old and die, and with them die their ideas.
>
> Instead of burning the heretic at the stake, we may benefit more if we listen to him and carefully observe whether his ideas bear good fruit or

not. If his message is not holy, it will fade away when subjected to the free competition of ideas. The open-minded approach is to look for God in a multitude of ways, in the kind of empirical questioning pursued by natural scientists and those theologians who recognize that some of tomorrow's spiritual heroes may be among those considered today as heretics.[6]

It is difficult not to see the strong element of pride and self-centeredness in both the atheistic scientist and the religious separatist. Both have excluded the possibility of other valid sources of truth. An attitude of humility would open their minds and hearts, freeing them to greater understanding. It would encourage a spirit of exploration, which for many potentially creative people is no longer considered an option. The arrogance of many scientists and religionists has led to the impression that everything is settled, that there are no frontiers left and no new worlds to conquer. Yet from what we have tried to share about the very limited degree of our present understanding in both science and religion, it should be evident that there is a whole universe to be explored. We have barely scratched the surface! In biological science, for example, the burgeoning fields of neural science and developmental genetics beckon with fascinating questions about the relationship between the mind and the brain, about the developments of the embryo and the mechanisms of macroevolution. In theology, the relationship between mankind and the rest of the created order need fresh study in light of the evidence of the recency of our origin and yet the closeness of our relationship to the rest of living things. Questions raised in behavior genetics and in environmental science offer tremendous and exciting challenges for the students of religion.

Scientists and theologians should see opportunity in a theology of humility to pool their resources and explore together the vast reaches of the universe. We take as our models those careful scientists who are not deluded by intellectual pride and who do not deny the metaphysical. Only arrogance would lead others to assert that what they cannot comprehend cannot exist. We see the opportunity for an integration of the disciplines of science and religion. The really paramount questions about our nature and the meaning of our pilgrimage are strongly interdisciplinary. Already science is demonstrating the fruitfulness of interdisciplinary studies in the relatively new field of neural science and the very new field of cognitive science. We forecast tremendous advances in human understanding and development when humble scientists and theologians meet together in joint interdisciplinary research, in a kind of experimental theology.

The future will be open to the scientific exploration of spiritual subjects such as love, prayer, meditation, and thanksgiving. This new exploration may reveal that there are spiritual laws, universal principles that operate in the spiritual domain, just as natural laws operate in the physical realm.

Such an experimental theology would be God-centered, recognizing the inadequacy of our senses and our intellect to comprehend the Creator, yet realizing that God also manifests himself through a spiritual dimension that not only speaks to each of us personally but seems to pervade the world we live in. Such an experimental theology will recognize that a new Renaissance in human knowledge is coming, building on the powerful insights of the past with new data from the physical and human sciences. This future religious emphasis will encourage thinking that is open-minded, and conclusions that are tentative. It will encourage diversity rather than syncretism, even as our universe has proved to be in constant change and progressive development.

With this new sense of humility, the way is now open to examine scientifically the spiritual nature of human beings. Indeed, several researchers have already begun an extensive examination of religious variables in health care. Of special significance is the work of psychiatrist David Larson and his colleagues in revealing the extent to which religious commitment is ignored or mismeasured in clinical medicine,[7] and the work of Herbert Benson, author of the best-selling book, *The Relaxation Response.*[8] Benson, the director of the Mind-Body Medical Institute at Harvard Medical School and the New England Deaconess Hospital, is conducting research into the relationship between spirituality and health that demonstrates that spiritual experience is correlated with increased life purpose and satisfaction, a health-promoting attitude, and decreased frequency of medical symptoms.[9]

Several institutions are developing programs along these lines. The National Institute for Healthcare Research in Arlington, Virginia, is pressing forward with studies that include an examination of religious values in family life, and the John Templeton Foundation of Bryn Mawr, Pennsylvania, is developing a broad program to encourage experimental and statistical study of spiritual entities such as love, prayer, forgiveness, and thanksgiving. The foundation has established a Center for Humility Theology, devoted to the encouragement of scientific research into the spiritual realm based upon the open and humble attitude engendered among theologians and scientists by the new discoveries of science.

Interest is already increased among research scientists. Nobel laureate Sir John Eccles and MIT's Institute Professor Emeritus Frances O. Schmitt, both pioneer neurophysiologists, have taken leadership roles in promoting research into the spiritual realm. Schmitt, who was the organizer of the Neural Sciences Research Program in 1962 that has now grown into the fifteen-thousand-member Society for Neuroscience, has recently called for a new research program to study the mind-brain-spirit relationship and parapsychological phenomena such as psychokenesis and extrasensory perception with the same rigor and enthusiasm that has been applied to the study of brain mechanisms.[10]

Perhaps the future will see research foundations and religious institutions devoting huge resources to spiritual research just as today we provide enormous amounts of funding for research into physical health. There would be great rewards in terms of increased human peace, harmony, happiness, and productivity as evidence accumulates that mankind's spiritual nature is the central aspect of our being.

Finally, if reality eludes us because it is deeper and more profound than we can ever truly comprehend, because it is an expression of the God of the universe, then it should be our finest goal to know God by every avenue open to us. Surely the best and most profound studies in all of history will come when performed humbly with the expectation of more fully knowing the Creator God and his purposes for his creatures.

The Old Testament prophet Micah left us a most salient exhortation:

And what does the Lord require of you?
To act justly and to love mercy
And to walk humbly with your God.[11]

Endnotes

Introduction

1. Arthur Peacocke, *Intimations of Reality; Critical Realism in Science and Religion* (Notre Dame, Ind.: University of Notre Dame Press, 1984), p.13.
2. George Field and Eric Chaisson, *The Invisible Universe* (Boston: Birkhauser, 1985), p. xi.
3. Loren Eiseley, *The Immense Journey* (New York: Vintage Books, Random House, 1957), p. 210.

Chapter 1

1. Peacocke, *Intimations of Reality*, p. 16.
2. Mary Hess, *Revolutions and Reconstructions in the Philosophy of Science* (Brighton: Harvester Press, 1981), p. xii.
3. Thomas Kuhn, *The Structure of Scientific Revolutions*, 2nd edition (Chicago: University of Chicago Press, 1970), p. 206.
4. Peacocke, *Intimations of Reality*, p. 18.
5. Ernan McMullin, "The Relativist Critique of Science," in *The Sciences and Theology in the Twentieth Century*, ed. Arthur Peacocke (Notre Dame, Ind.: University of Notre Dame Press, 1981), pp. 301-2.
6. Ernan McMullin, "A Case for Scientific Realism," in *Scientific Realism*, ed. Jarrett Leplin (Berkeley: University of California Press, 1984), pp. 30, 31.
7. Michael Polanyi, *Personal Knowledge: An Introduction to Post-Critical Philosophy* (New York: Harper and Row, 1966).
8. John Templeton and Robert Herrmann, *The God Who Would Be Known* (New York: Harper and Row, 1989).
9. McMullin, "A Case for Scientific Realism," p. 26.
10. Peacocke, *Intimations of Reality*, p. 26
11. Ibid., p. 27.
12. Ibid., p. 28.
13. Ian Hacking, *Representing and Intervening* (Cambridge: Cambridge University Press, 1983), p. 275.
14. Richard Morris, *The Nature of Reality* (New York: Noonday Press, Farrar Straus and Giroux, 1987), pp. 112-13.

15. Peacocke, *Intimations of Reality*, p. 30.

16. Janet Soskice, *Metaphor and Religious Language* (Oxford: Clarendon Press, paperback edition, 1987), p. 115.

17. Peacocke, *Intimations of Reality*, pp. 23, 32.

18. Morris, *The Nature of Reality*, p. 193.

19. Ibid., pp. 193-94.

20. Ibid., p. 194.

21. Stephen Hawking, *A Brief History of Time* (Toronto: Bantam Books, 1988).

22. Morris, *The Nature of Reality*, pp. 175, 194-95.

23. Ibid., p. 176.

24. Ibid., pp. 178, 179.

25. Ibid., pp. 176, 195.

26. Arthur Peacocke, *God and the New Biology* (San Fransisco: Harper and Row, 1986).

27. Donald MacKay, *The Clockwork Image* (Downers Grove, Ill.: InterVarsity Press, 1974), pp. 44-45.

28. Peacocke, *God and the New Biology*, pp. 21, 22, 25.

29. François Jacob, *The Logic of Living Systems* (London: Allen Lane, 1974), pp. 302, 406-7.

30. Peacocke, *Intimations of Reality*, pp. 35-36.

31. Peacocke, *God and the New Biology*, p. 28.

32. William James, *The Varieties of Religious Experience* (New York: Longmans, 1902).

33. Alistair Hardy, *The Spiritual Nature of Man* (Oxford: Oxford University Press, 1979).

34. Polanyi, *Personal Knowledge*.

35. Lincoln Barnet, *The Universe and Dr. Einstein* (New York: Signet, 1948), p. 118.

36. Werner Heisenberg, *Physics and Beyond* (New York: Harper and Row, 1978), pp. 214-17.

37. Loren Eiseley, *The Firmament of Time* (New York: Atheneum, 1985), p. 113.

38. Templeton and Herrmann, *The God Who Would Be Known*, chap. 8.

39. Peacocke, *Intimations of Reality* , p. 38

40. Ibid., p. 40.

41. Ian Ramsey, *Models and Mystery, Models for Divine Activity, and Religious Language* (London: SCM Press, 1957).

42. Peacocke, *Intimations of Reality*, p. 42. See also Peacocke, *Science and the Christian Experiment* (London: Oxford University Press, 1971), pp. 12-28.

43. Peacocke *Intimations of Reality*, p. 37.

44. Ibid., pp. 43-44. See also T. Fawcett, *The Symbolic Language of Religion* (London: SCM Press, 1970).

45. Soskice, *Metaphor and Religious Language*, p. 112.

46. Peacocke, *Intimations of Reality*, p. 47.

47. Thomas F. Torrance, "Realism and Openness in Scientific Inquiry," *Zygon* 23 (1988): 166.

48. Edward O. Wilson, *Sociobiology, the New Synthesis* (Cambridge: Belknap, 1975), pp. 5-6.

49. Philip Hefner, "Is/Ought: A Risky Relationship between Theology and Science," in *The Sciences and Theology in the Twentieth Century,* ed. A.R. Peacocke (Notre Dame, Ind.: University of Notre Dame Press, 1981).

50. Thomas F. Torrance, "Theology and Science," Center of Theological Inquiry Consultation (Princeton, N.J., October 1988).

Chapter 2

1. Morris, *The Nature of Reality,* pp. 62, 195.
2. Ibid., pp. 16-21.
3. Robert Crease and Charles Mann, "How the Universe Works," *Atlantic Monthly* (August 1984): 68-69.
4. Morris, *The Nature of Reality,* p. 53.
5. Crease and Mann, "How the Universe Works," p. 70.
6. Ibid., p. 78.
7. Morris, *The Nature of Reality,* p. 73.
8. Ibid., pp. 74-78.
9. Ibid., pp. 80-81.
10. Ibid., p. 81.

Chapter 3

1. Robert P. Crease and Charles C. Mann, *The Second Creation* (New York: Macmillan, 1986), p. 412.
2. Timothy Ferris, *Coming of Age in the Milky Way* (New York: Willam Morrow, 1988), pp. 185-86.
3. Thomas Torrance, *A Dynamical Theory of the Electromagnetic Field* (Edinburgh: Scottish Academic Press, 1982), p. x.
4. Ibid.
5. Ferris, *Coming of Age in the Milky Way,* p. 298.
6. Ibid., 298-99.
7. Ibid., p. 299.
8. Ibid., pp. 301-7.
9. Crease and Mann, *The Second Creation,* pp. 189-90.
10. Ibid., pp. 190-91.
11. Ferris, *Coming of Age in the Milky Way,* p. 310.
12. Ibid., p. 313.
13. Ibid., pp. 319-21.
14. Philip J. Hilts, *Scientific Temperaments* (New York: Simon & Schuster, 1982) p. 86.
15. Ferris, *Coming of Age in the Milky Way,* pp. 320-21.
16. Hawking, *A Brief History of Time,* pp. 71-72.
17. Ibid.
18. Ibid., p. 74.
19. Ibid., p. 75.
20. Crease and Mann, "How the Universe Works," p. 92.
21. Ferris, *Coming of Age in the Milky Way,* p. 327.
22. Crease and Mann, *The Second Creation,* p. 411.
23. Ibid., p. 415.

24. Ferris, *Coming of Age in the Milky Way*, p. 328.

25. Crease and Mann, *The Second Creation*, pp. 415-17.

26. Ferris, *Coming of Age in the Milky Way*, p. 333.

27. Ibid., pp. 333-34.

28. Crease and Mann, *The Second Creation*, pp. 417-18.

29. Ferris, *Coming of Age in the Milky Way*, p. 334.

30. Ibid., p. 338.

31. Ibid., pp. 338-40.

32. Ibid., p. 341.

33. Ibid., p. 346.

34. Hawking, *A Brief History of Time*, pp. 83-87.

35. Ibid., pp. 50-51.

36. Ibid., p. 133.

37. Ferris, *Coming of Age in the Milky Way*, pp. 363-64.

38. Ibid., p. 364.

39. Hawking, *A Brief History of Time*, pp. 137-38.

40. Ibid., p. 138.

41. Ibid., p. 139.

42. Ibid.

43. Ferris, *Coming of Age in the Milky Way*, p. 364.

44. Hawking, *A Brief History of Time*, pp. 140-41.

45. Ferris, *Coming of Age in the Milky Way*, p. 383.

Chapter 4

1. Paul Davies, *The Cosmic Blueprint* (New York: Simon & Schuster, 1988), p. 2.

2. Freeman Dyson, *Infinite in All Directions* (New York: Harper & Row, 1988).

3. Ibid., p. 6.

4. Ibid., p. 21.

5. Ibid., p. 36.

6. Ibid., pp. 37-47.

7. Davies, *The Cosmic Blueprint*, p. 5.

8. Ibid., p. 203.

9. Ibid., p. 14.

10. Ilya Prigogine and Isabelle Stengers, *Order out of Chaos* (New York: Bantam Books, 1984).

11. Arthur Fisher, "Chaos, the Ultimate Asymmetry," *Mosaic* 16 (January-February 1985): 26.

12. Davies, *The Cosmic Blueprint*, pp. 22-23.

13. Prigogine and Stengers, *Order out of Chaos*, p. 143.

14. Davies, *The Cosmic Blueprint*, p. 42.

15. Ibid., pp. 52-54.

16. Ilya Prigogine, *From Being to Becoming: Time and Complexity in the Physical Sciences* (San Francisco: Freeman, 1980), p. 214.

17. Davies, *The Cosmic Blueprint*, pp. 55-56.

18. Ibid., p. 121.

19. Ibid., pp. 138-39.
20. Ibid., p. 140.
21. Henri Bergson *Creative Evolution*, trans. A. Mitchell (London: Macmillan, 1964), p. 255.
22. Karl Popper and John Eccles, *The Self and Its Brain* (Berlin: Springer International, 1977), pp. 14-15.
23. Davies, *The Cosmic Blueprint*, p. 141.
24. Ibid., p. 142.
25. Ibid., p. 143.
26. Donald MacKay, *Science and Christian Faith Today* (London: CPA's Publications, 1960), pp. 8-9.
27. Ibid., pp. 9-11.

Chapter 5

1. J. D. Watson, *The Double Helix* (New York: Atheneum, 1968).
2. M. Nirenberg and J. Matthai, "The Dependence of Cell-Free Protein Synthesis in *E. Coli* upon Naturally Occuring or Synthetic Polyribonucleotides," *Proceedings of the National Academy of Science*, US 47 (1961): 1588.
3. J. Lucas-Lenard and F. Lipmann, "Protein Biosynthesis," *Annual Review of Biochemistry* 40 (1971): 409.
4. R. Herrmann, "Genesis and Biogenesis," *Christian Medical Society Journal* (Winter 1970): 10-17.
5. Davies, *The Cosmic Blueprint*, pp. 116-17.
6. H. Quastler, *The Emergence of Biological Organization* (New Haven: Yale University Press, 1964), pp. 7-16.
7. J. Roth, *Bulletin of the Institute of Cellular Biology*, Univ. of Connecticut, 8 (1966).
8. C. R. Woese, "The Emergence of Genetic Organization," in *Exobiology*, C. Ponnamperuma, ed., *Frontiers in Biology*, vol. 23 (1972): 318-27.
9. S. R. Pelac and M.G.E. Welton, "Steriochemical Relationship between Coding Triplets and Amino Acids," *Nature* 209 (1966): 868-70.
10. R. Shapiro, *Origins—Skeptic's Guide to the Creation of Life on Earth* (New York: Summit Books, 1983), pp. 266-80.
11. C. Thaxton, W. Bradley, and R. Olsen, *The Mystery of Life's Origin: Reassessing Current Theories* (New York: Philosophical Library, 1984).
12. D. Kenyon and G. Steinman, *Biochemical Predestination* (New York: McGraw Hill, 1969).
13. Thaxton et al., *Mystery of Life's Origin*, pp. v-vii.
14. Ibid., p. 186.
15. Dyson, *Infinite in All Directions*, pp. 54-73.
16. Ibid., p. 55.
17. Ibid., p. 68.
18. L. Margolis, *Symbiosis in Cell Evolution* (San Francisco: Freeman & Co., 1981).
19. F. Dyson, *Infinite in All Directions*, p. 69.
20. A. Oparin, *The Origin of Life*, 3rd edition, translated by Ann Synge (Edinburgh: Oliver & Boyd, 1924).

21. F. Dyson, *Infinite in All Directions*, p. 83.

22. Ibid., pp. 84–85.

23. Ibid., p. 90.

24. Ibid., p. 91.

25. Ibid., p. 92.

26. R. Dawkins, *The Selfish Gene* (New York: Oxford University Press, 1976).

27. Dyson, *Infinite in All Directions*, pp. 93-95.

28. E. O. Wilson, remarks quoted by R. Lewin in *Science* 216 (1982): 1091-92.

29. J. Polkinghorne, *Science and Creation: The Search for Understanding* (Boston: New Science Library, 1989) pp. 51-53.

30. Davies, *The Cosmic Blueprint*, pp. 118-20.

31. L. Young, *The Unfinished Universe* (New York: Simon & Schuster, 1986), pp. 61-63.

32. Davies, *The Cosmic Blueprint*, p. 119.

33. Eiseley, *The Immense Journey*, pp. 26-27, 210.

Chapter 6

1. Young, *The Unfinished Universe*, pp. 75-84.

2. Ibid., p. 57.

3. Ibid., p. 76.

4. L. Margolis, *Symbiosis in Cell Evolution* (San Francisco: Freeman & Company, 1961).

5. Young, *The Unfinished Universe*, p. 81.

6. D. Price, J. Wieter and W. Hearn, *Teaching Science in a Climate of Controversy* (Ipswich, Mass.: American Scientific Affiliation, 1986), p. 34.

7. S. Gould, *Wonderful Life—the Burgess Shale and the Nature of History* (New York: W. W. Norton & Co., 1989).

8. Young, *The Unfinished Universe*, p. 84.

9. Ibid., p. 87.

10. Ibid., p. 89.

11. Gould, *Wonderful Life*, p. 99.

12. L. Margolis and K. Schwartz, *Five Kingdoms* (San Francisco: W. H. Freeman, 1982).

13. Eiseley, *The Immense Journey*

14. Ibid., p. 64.

15. Ibid., p. 73.

16. Ibid., p. 77.

17. Gould, *Wonderful Life*.

18. Ibid., p. 24.

19. Ibid., p. 24-25.

20. Ibid., p. 227.

21. Ibid., p. 230.

22. J. Valentine, "General Patterns in Metazoan Evolution," in A Hallam, ed., *Patterns of Evolution* (New York: Elsevier Science Publishers, 1977).

23. Gould, *Wonderful Life*, p. 234.

24. Ibid., pp. 238-39.

25. Young, *The Unfinished Universe*, p. 96.

26. E. Sinnott, *The Biology of the Spirit* (New York: Viking Press, 1955), pp. 32-36.

27. Young, *The Unfinished Universe*, pp. 104-5.

28. L. Thomas, *The Lives of a Cell* (New York: Viking Press, 1974), p. 145.

29. J. Lovelock, *Gaia: A New Look at Life on Earth* (Oxford: Oxford University Press, 1979).

30. Young, *The Unfinished Universe*, p. 92.

31. J. Huxley, *Evolution: The Modern Synthesis* (New York: Harper & Row, 1942).

32. Young, *The Unfinished Universe*, p. 91.

33. J. Polkinghorne, *Science and Creation* (Boston: New Science Library, 1988).

34. J. Monod, *Chance and Necessity* (New York: Collins, 1972).

35. Polkinghorne, *Science and Creation*, pp. 47-48.

36. J. Polkinghorne, *The Quantum World* (London: Longmans, 1984), pp. 11-12.

37. J. Polkinghorne, *Science and Creation*, p. 49.

38. Ibid., p. 49.

39. Ibid., p. 52.

40. Ibid., p. 61.

41. Ibid., p. 62.

42. W. H. Vanstone, *Love's Endeavor, Love's Expense* (Darton: Longman and Todd, 1977), pp. 62-63.

Chapter 7

1. R. Lewin, *In the Age of Mankind* (Washington, D.C.: Smithsonian Books, 1988).

2. Ibid., p. 19.

3. Ibid.

4. D. Wilcox, personal communication.

5. Lewin, *In the Age of Mankind*, p. 20.

6. Gould, *Wonderful Life*, pp. 276-77.

7. Lewin *In the Age of Mankind*, p. 47.

8. Ibid., p. 61.

9. K. W. Weaver "The Search for Our Ancestors" *National Geographic* 168 (1985): p. 578.

10. Ibid., p. 589.

11. Lewin, *In the Age of Mankind*, pp. 81-85.

12. Weaver, "The Search for Our Ancestors," p. 599.

13. Ibid., p. 585.

14. Lewin, *In the Age of Mankind*, p. 59.

15. K. Weaver, "The Search for Our Ancestors," pp. 588-89.

16. Ibid., p. 589-90.

17. Lewin, *In the Age of Mankind*, p. 50.

18. Ibid., p. 57.

19. Ibid.

20. R. Leakey and A. Walker, "Homo Erectus Unearthed," *National Geographic* 168 (1985): 625-29.

21. Lewin, *In the Age of Mankind*, p. 112.

22. Ibid., pp. 120-122.

23. Eiseley, *The Firmament of Time*, p. 113.

24. Lewin, *In the Age of Mankind*, p. 123.

25. Ibid., pp. 127-28.

26. C. B. Stringer, "The Emergence of Modern Humans," *Scientific American* (December 1990): 102-3.

27. Ibid., p. 99.

28. C. B. Stringer, R. Grun, H. P. Schwarcz, and P. Goldberg, "ESR Dates for the Hominid Burial Site of Es Skhul in Israel," *Nature* 338 (1989): 756-58.

29. H. Valladas, J. L. Reyss, J. L. Joron, G. Valladas, O. Bar-Joseph, and B. Vandermeersch, "Thioluminescence Dating of Mousterian Proto-Cro-Magnon Remains from Israel and the Origin of Modern Man," *Nature* 331 (1988).

30. Lewin, *In the Age of Mankind*, pp. 128-29.

31. Stringer, "The Emergence of Modern Humans," pp. 102-3.

32. D. Wilcox, "Created in Eternity, Unfolded in Time," manuscript in preparation, (St. Davids, Penn: Eastern College, 1990)., chap. 7, p. 11.

33. Ibid., chap. 7, p. 16.

34. Lewin, *In the Age of Mankind*, pp. 134-35, 137.

35. Ibid., pp. 139-42.

36. Ibid., pp. 144-45.

37. Ibid., p. 133.

38. Stringer, "The Emergence of Modern Humans."

39. J. J. Putnam, "The Search for Modern Humans," *National Geographic* 174 (1988): 463.

40. Wilcox, *Created in Eternity, Unfolded in Time*, chap. 7, pp. 2-4.

41. Ibid., chap. 7, p. 4.

42. Genesis 1:26, 27 Holy Bible, New International Version (Grand Rapids, Mich.: Zondervan, 1978).

43. C. G. Smith, *Ancestral Voices* (Englewood Cliffs, N.J.: Prentice Hall, 1985).

44. J. Goodall, "The Behavior of Free-living Chimpanzees in the Gombe Stream Reserve," *Animal Behavior Monographs* 1 (1968): 161-311.

45. Gould, *Wonderful Life*, p. 319.

46. J. Polkinghorne, *The Way the World Is* (Grand Rapids, Mich: Eerdmans, 1983), pp. 11-12.

47. T. S. Eliot, "Little Gidding," *The Complete Poems and Plays 1909-1950* (New York: Harcourt Brace & World, 1971), p. 145.

Chapter 8

1. Eiseley, *The Firmament of Time*, p. 5.

2. K. C. Cole, "On Imagining the Unseeable," *Discover* (December 1982): 70.

3. Templeton and Herrmann, *The God Who Would Be Known*.

4. J. Polkinghorne, *Reason and Reality* (London: SPCK, 1991), pp. 34-36.

5. Ibid., p. 36.

6. Ibid., pp. 37-38.

Chapter 9

1. Polanyi, *Personal Knowledge.*

2. Templeton and Herrmann, *The God Who Would Be Known,* pp. 22-23.

3. Ibid.

4. J. Bayly, *HIS Magazine*

5. Matthew 15:9, Holy Bible, King James Version.

6. J. Templeton, *The Humble Approach* (New York: Seabury Press, 1981), pp. 46, 51.

7. D. Larson, E. Patterson, D. Blazer, A. Omran, and B. Kaplan, "Systematic Analysis of Research on Religious Variables in Four Major Psychiatric Journals, 1978-1982," *American Journal of Psychiatry,* 143 (1986): 329-34. F. Craigie, D. Larson, and I. Liu, "References to Religion in the Journal of Family Practice," *Journal of Family Practice,* 30 (1990): 477.

8. H. Benson, *The Relaxation Response* (New York: William Morrow, 1975).

9. J. Kass, R. Friedman, J. Leserman, P. Zuttermeister, and H. Benson, "Health Outcomes and a New Index of Spiritual Experience," *Journal for the Scientific Study of Religion,* in press. S. Myers and H. Benson, "Psychological Factors in Healing: A New Perspective on an Old Debate," *Behavioral Medicine* 18 (1992): 5-11.

10. F. O. Schmitt, "Generating a New Paradigm in the Context of Science and Theology," Templeton Foundation Symposium, "Human Viability and a World Theology" (Chicago, Ill.: Chicago Center for Religion and Science, November 16, 1991).

11. Micah 6:8, Holy Bible, New International Version (Grand Rapids, Mich.: Zondervan, 1978).

Index